AN INTRODUCTION TO VALUE-AT-RISK

Fourth Edition

The Securities & Investment Institute

Mission Statement:

To set standards of professional excellence and integrity for the investment and securities industry, providing qualifications and promoting the highest level of competence to our members, other individuals and firms.

The Securities and Investment Institute is the UK's leading professional and membership body for practitioners in the securities and investment industry, with more than 16,000 members with an increasing number working outside the UK. It is also the major examining body for the industry, with a full range of qualifications aimed at people entering and working in it. More than 30,000 examinations are taken annually in more than 30 countries.

You can contact us through our website *www.sii.org.uk*

Our membership believes that keeping up to date is central to professional development. We are delighted to endorse the Wiley/SII publishing partnership and recommend this series of books to our members and all those who work in the industry.

Ruth Martin
Managing Director

AN INTRODUCTION TO VALUE-AT-RISK

Fourth Edition

Moorad Choudhry

JOHN WILEY & SONS, LTD

Published in 2006 by John Wiley & Sons Ltd, The Atrium, Southern Gate, Chichester,
West Sussex PO19 8SQ, England

Telephone (+44) 1243 779777

Email (for orders and customer service enquiries): cs-books@wiley.co.uk
Visit our Home Page on www.wiley.com

Other Wiley Editorial Offices

John Wiley & Sons, Inc., 111 River Street, Hoboken, NJ 07030, USA

Jossey-Bass, 989 Market Street, San Francisco, CA 94103-1741, USA

Wiley-VCH Verlag GmbH, Boschstr. 12, D-69469 Weinheim, Germany

John Wiley & Sons Australia Ltd, 42 McDougall Street, Milton, Queensland 4064, Australia

John Wiley & Sons (Asia) Pte Ltd, 2 Clementi Loop #02-01, Jin Xing Distripark, Singapore 129809

John Wiley & Sons Canada Ltd, 22 Worcester Road, Etobicoke, Ontario, Canada M9W 1L1

Wiley also publishes its books in a variety of electronic formats. Some content that appears
in print may not be available in electronic books.

British Library Cataloguing in Publication Data

A catalogue record for this book is available from the British Library

ISBN-13 978-0-470-01757-9 (PB)
ISBN-10 0-470-01757-0 (PB)

Project management by Originator, Gt Yarmouth, Norfolk (typeset in 10/12pt Trump Mediaeval).
Printed and bound in Great Britain by T.J. International Ltd, Padstow, Cornwall.
This book is printed on acid-free paper responsibly manufactured from sustainable forestry
in which at least two trees are planted for each one used for paper production.

To Rod Pienaar
This time next year, we'll be millionaires ...

CONTENTS

FOREWORD

. . . .

In today's financial environment, and reflecting high-profile market events over the years such as the collapse of Barings, Orange County, and Enron, we continue to see a far greater focus on all areas of Risk Management. One simple measure of this increasing interest is the growth and focus in the number of risk professionals in today's rapidly changing environment. This increase also reflects the commonly held view that risk management is an integral and indispensable part of any financial organisation today.

Within the Market Risk arena, there are a number of skills required to fulfil your role effectively which are common requirements in most jobs, such as general knowledge about your product area, analytical skills and an intuitive analytical capability to name but a few. Leading on from this, some of the more useful 'tools of the trade' within Risk Management include, for instance, knowledge of financial instruments and how they trade; this for cash as well as derivative instruments such as options. But these remain as components of the bigger picture overall. The VaR measure is a fundamental tool within Market Risk Management, and practitioners need to be familiar with it as a concept and its various measurement methodologies. Of course, we must remember that it should not be solely relied upon, but used in conjunction with other tools when managing financial risk.

VaR is one of the simplest measures of financial risk there is and is calculated in many different ways by each individual institution. It is useful therefore that the scope of this book has been aimed towards providing an extensive and broad-based awareness about VaR overall, rather than overwhelming you with the mathematics behind the VaR methodology of each institution in the marketplace.

If you do not have any prior knowledge of VaR or Risk Management, this book is perfect for an entry into this arena and provides a solid basis for further research towards understanding more about Risk Management.

Ketul Tanna
Market Risk Management
JPMorgan Chase Bank
London

PREFACE

....

In 1998 I put together an introductory course on Value-at-Risk for the Securities Institute in London, at the invitation of Zena Doidge. This was a departure for me: my background and work experience up to then had not been in risk management; I had spent the previous 6 years as a bond and money markets trader. However, due to personal circumstances I found myself in the position of teaching courses on various bond market subjects. This particular course forced me to actually research the topic though, and not just rely on my work experience as I might have done when I taught a course on (say) swaps or repo. Thus began an interest in writing, more specifically writing incorporating research and academic rigour rather than just practical experience. Anyway, I delivered the course in June or July that year and it seemed to go down okay. Then Zena suggested that the course companion that I had produced for the course might make a useful textbook on the subject. I had not thought at all about doing this, but as it happened the Institute had its own publishing arm, so there was no need for me to go out and try to get a publishing deal! Thus, my first ever book was born, which came out in March 1999. And here we are with the fourth edition of that book, now with John Wiley & Sons in Chichester and destined to be, or so I assure myself, my last book.

The world of capital markets is very fast-moving, and risk management is no different. Much has happened since the first edition was published, both in terms of new products and processes and in terms of significant events that have tested the resilience and liquidity of the markets as a whole. From the point of view of the risk management practitioner, the key concern is the need to keep up with market developments and also to update procedures such that the tools of his trade, such as the value-at-risk measurement method, remain effective. We hope we have captured some of these latest developments in this book.

As well as a general update, the main difference in this fourth edition from the previous editions is a re-ordering of chapters so that some of the appendices now appear in the main body of the text. This is because in hindsight we feel that a grounding in these subjects is important in any introduction to VaR. Some new features include:

- an illustration of portfolio VaR using Bloomberg sceens;
- more detail in the existing chapters on fixed income instruments and options;
- an introduction to Monte Carlo simulation and VaR.

Last but we hope not least, Chapter 8 on credit VaR has been enlarged with discussion on credit ratings migration and risk measurement for credit derivatives. But we remain true to the spirit of the first edition: that is, as befits a book directed at newcomers to the market, material is kept simple and accessible throughout.

Moorad Choudhry
Surrey, England
March 2006

PREFACE TO THE FIRST
EDITION

· ·

The concept of Value-at-Risk (VaR) has become a mainstay of financial markets risk management since its introduction by JP Morgan in 1994. An increasing number of banks and securities houses, and corporates, now use VaR as their main tool for providing management information on the size of their risk exposure. Initially VaR was used to measure the extent of market risk exposure; this was followed by the application of VaR methodology to the measurement of credit risk exposure.

As this is an introduction to the subject we have attempted to place VaR in context; hence the book begins by defining risk and describing the risk management function and other tools of risk measurement in the financial markets. VaR is best viewed as a tool within an overall risk management framework and hopefully the contents within will communicate this to the reader. An integrated risk management function within a bank or securities house will wish to incorporate VaR as part of its overall risk exposure and control framework. When such a framework is effective it serves an important purpose in providing comfort to a firm's shareholders that the management of trading, market and credit risk is no longer a significant cause for concern. At this point VaR as a risk measurement tool might be said to have come of age, and perhaps have assisted in the realisation of shareholder value.

This book has been written for those with little or no previous understanding of or exposure to the concept of risk management and Value-at-Risk; however it also describes the subject in sufficient depth to be of use as a reference to a more experienced practitioner. It is primarily aimed at front office, middle office and back office banking and fund management staff who are involved to some extent in risk management. Others including corporate and local authority treasurers may wish to refer to the contents. Undergraduate and postgraduate students and MBA students specialising in financial markets will also find this book useful as a reference text. Comments on the text should be sent to the author care of the Securities Institute Services.

ACKNOWLEDGEMENTS
First edition

Parts of this book were originally written for the introductory course on Value-at-Risk run by the Securities Institute in London. My thanks to Zena Doidge at the Institute, whom it was a pleasure to work with, for giving me the opportunity to teach this course. Thanks to Debra Maddison in the Institute's publishing department, and Simon Chapman for graphics help.

I would also like to thank Richard Thornton at KPMG for lending me his book on VaR.

Third edition

Thanks to Kalbinder Dhillon at the Securities Institute for graphics help.

Fourth edition

Love, affection and respect to Paul Claxton, Harry Cross, Abukar Ali, Didier Joannas, Khurram Butt, Michael Nicoll, Mo Dualeh, Phil Broadhurst, and all those to whom I want to tell that it's a privilege to call my friends.

Nothing lasts forever. But then again, some things never change . . .

ABOUT THE AUTHOR

Moorad Choudhry is Head of Treasury at KBC Financial Products in London. He joined there from JPMorgan Chase Bank, where he was a vice-president in Structured Finance Services sales and marketing. Prior to that he was a sterling proprietary trader in the Treasury division at Hambros Bank Limited, and at ABN Amro Hoare Govett Sterling Bonds Limited where he ran the short-dated gilts and money markets desk. He began his City career at the London Stock Exchange in 1989. He was educated at Claremont Fan Court school in Esher, Surrey, the University of Westminster, University of Reading, Henley Management College and Birkbeck, University of London.

Dr Choudhry is a Visiting Professor at the Department of Economics, London Metropolitan University, a Visiting Research Fellow at the ICMA Centre, University of Reading, a Senior Fellow at the Centre for Mathematical Trading and Finance, Cass Business School, a Fellow of the Global Association of Risk Professionals, a Fellow of the Institute of Sales and Marketing Management, and a Fellow of the Securities and Investment Institute.

Chapter

1

....

INTRODUCTION TO RISK

The risk management department was one of the fastest growing areas in investment and commercial banks during the 1990s. A string of high-profile banking losses and failures, typified by the fall of Barings Bank in 1995, highlighted the importance of risk management to bank managers and shareholders alike. In response to the volatile and complex nature of risks that they were exposed to, banks set up specialist risk management departments, whose functions included both measuring and managing risk. As a value-added function, risk management can assist banks not only in managing risk, but also in understanding the nature of their profit and loss, and so help increase return on capital. It is now accepted that senior directors of banks need to be thoroughly familiar with the concept of risk management. One of the primary tools of the risk manager is *value-at-risk (VaR)*, which is a quantitative measure of the risk exposure of an institution. For a while VaR was regarded as somewhat inaccessible, and only the preserve of mathematicians and quantitative analysts. Although VaR is indeed based on statistical techniques that may be difficult to grasp for the layman, its basic premise can be explained in straightforward fashion, in a way that enables non-academics to become comfortable with the concept. Later in the book we describe and explain the calculation and application of VaR. We begin here with a discussion of risk.

DEFINING RISK

Any transaction or undertaking with an element of uncertainty as to its future outcome carries an element of risk: risk can be thought of as uncertainty. To associate particular assets such as equities, bonds or corporate cash flows with types of risk, we need to define 'risk' itself. It is useful to define risk in terms of a risk *horizon*, the point at which an asset will be realised, or turned into cash. All market participants, including speculators, have an horizon, which may be as short as a half-day. Essentially then, the horizon is the time period relating to the risk being considered.

Once we have established a notion of horizon, a working definition of risk is *the uncertainty of the future total cash value of an investment on the investor's horizon date.* This uncertainty arises from many sources. For participants in the financial markets risk is essentially a measure of the volatility of asset returns, although it has a broader definition as being any type of uncertainty as to future outcomes. The types of risk that a bank or securities house is exposed to as part of its operations in the bond and capital markets are characterised below.

THE ELEMENTS OF RISK: CHARACTERISING RISK

Banks and other financial institutions are exposed to a number of risks during the course of normal operations. The different types of risk are broadly characterised as follows:

- *Market risk* – risk arising from movements in prices in financial markets. Examples include foreign exchange (*FX*) risk, interest rate risk and basis risk.
- *Credit risk* – something called *issuer risk* refers to risk that a customer will default. Examples include sovereign risk, marginal risk and *force majeure* risk.
- *Liquidity risk* – this refers to two different but related issues: for a Treasury or money markets' person, it is the risk that a bank has insufficient funding to meet commitments as they arise. That is, the risk that funds cannot be raised in the market as and when required. For a securities or derivatives trader, it is the risk that the market for assets becomes too thin to enable fair and efficient trading to take place. This is the risk that assets cannot be sold or bought as and when required.
- *Operational risk* – risk of loss associated with non-financial matters such as fraud, system failure, accidents and ethics. Table 1.1 assigns sources of risk for a range of fixed interest, FX, interest rate derivative and equity products. The classification has assumed a 1-year horizon, but the concepts apply to virtually any horizon.

Forms of market risk

Market risk reflects the uncertainty as to an asset's price when it is sold. Market risk is the risk arising from movements in financial market prices. Specific market risks will differ according to the type of asset under consideration:

Table 1.1 Characterising risk.

	Market	Reinvestment	Credit	Sovereign	FX	Basis	Performance	Prepayment
Government bond								
Developed country	▨							
Developing country	▨	▨	▨	▨				
Zero-coupon bond	▨		▨					
Corporate bond	▨	▨	▨					
Asset-backed bond	▨		▨					▨
Bank deposit	▨		▨					▨
FRA	▨		▨					
Futures contract	▨							
Forward contract			▨		▨			
Interest rate swap	▨							
Repo	▨	▨	▨					
Equity (listed exchange)	▨	▨	▨					

- *Currency risk* – this arises from exposure to movements in FX rates. Currency risk is often sub-divided into *transaction* risk, where currency fluctuations affect the proceeds from day-to-day transactions, and *translation* risk, which affects the value of assets and liabilities on a balance sheet.
- *Interest rate risk* – this arises from the impact of fluctuating interest rates and will directly affect any entity borrowing or investing funds. The most common exposure is simply to the level of interest rates but some institutions run positions that are exposed to changes in the shape of the yield curve. The basic risk arises from revaluation of the asset after a change in rates.

- *Equity risk* – this affects anyone holding a portfolio of shares, which will rise and fall with the level of individual share prices and the level of the stock market.
- *Other market risk* – there are residual market risks which fall in this category. Among these are *volatility* risk, which affects option traders, and *basis* risk, which has a wider impact. Basis risk arises whenever one kind of risk exposure is hedged with an instrument that behaves in a similar, but not necessarily identical manner. One example would be a company using 3-month interest rate futures to hedge its commercial paper (*CP*) programme. Although eurocurrency rates, to which futures prices respond, are well correlated with CP rates, they do not invariably move in lock step. If CP rates moved up by 50 basis points but futures prices dropped by only 35 basis points, the 15-bps gap would be the basis risk in this case.

Other risks

- *Liquidity risk* – this is the potential risk arising when an entity cannot meet payments when they fall due. It may involve borrowing at an excessive rate of interest, facing penalty payments under contractual terms, or selling assets at below market prices (*forced sale* risk). It also refers to an inability to trade or obtain a price when desired, due to lack of supply or demand or shortage of market-makers.
- *Counterparty risk* – all transactions involve one or both parties in counterparty risk, the potential loss that can arise if one party were to default on its obligations. Another name for counterparty risk is 'credit risk'. Every non-government backed investment carries the risk that its obligations might not be honoured.
- *Reinvestment risk* – if an asset makes any payments before the investor's horizon, whether it matures or not, the cash flows will have to be reinvested until the horizon date. Since the reinvestment rate is unknown when the asset is purchased, the final cash flow is uncertain.
- *Sovereign risk* – this is a type of credit risk specific to a government bond. There is minimal risk of default by an industrialised country. A developing country may default on its obligation (or declare a debt 'moratorium') if debt payments relative to domestic product reach unsustainable levels.

- *Prepayment risk* – this is specific to mortgage-backed and asset-backed bonds. For example, mortgage lenders allow the home-owner to repay outstanding debt before the stated maturity. If interest rates fall prepayment will occur, which forces reinvestment at rates lower than the initial yield.
- *Performance risk* – performance is a relatively new risk source, since it relates primarily to over-the-counter (*OTC*) derivative instruments. It would apply, for instance, to financial agreements that do not involve an extension of credit; little or no cash is exchanged at the agreement's inception. Instead, the contract calls for counterparties to exchange cash payments on a preset future date, according to a schedule based on the values of specific assets or indices. Since no loan of money has taken place, a 'default' by one of the counterparties does not mean that the 'funds extended' will not be returned. However, it is an extension of the notion of credit risk.
- *Model risk* – some of the latest financial instruments are heavily dependent on complex mathematical models for pricing and hedging. If the model is incorrectly specified, is based on questionable assumptions or does not accurately reflect the true behaviour of the market, banks trading these instruments could suffer extensive losses.

Risk estimation

There are a number of different ways of approaching the estimation of market risk. The key factors determining the approach are the user's response to two questions:

- Can the user accept the assumption of normality – is it reasonable to assume that market movements follow the normal distribution? If so, statistical tools can be employed.
- Does the value of positions change linearly with changes in market prices? If not (as is typical for option positions where market movements are not very small), simulation techniques will be more useful.

Were the answers to both questions to be 'yes' then we could be comfortable using standard measures of risk such as duration and convexity (these concepts are covered later). If the answers are 'no' then we are forced to use scenario analysis combined with simulation techniques. If, as is more likely, the answer to the first question is 'yes' and the second 'no', then a combination of statistical tools and simulation techniques will be required.

For most banks and securities houses the portfolio will almost certainly behave in a non-linear manner due to the use of options. Hence, a combination of statistical tools and simulation is likely to be the most effective risk measurement approach. The scenarios used in simulations are often a mixture of observed rate and price changes from selected periods in the past, and judgement calls by the risk manager. The various alternative methods are examined in Chapter 3.

RISK MANAGEMENT

The risk management function grew steadily in size and importance within commercial and investment banks during the 1990s. Risk management departments exist not to eliminate the possibility of all unexpected losses, should such action indeed be feasible or desirable; rather, to control the frequency, extent and size of such losses in such a way as to provide the minimum surprise to senior management and shareholders.

Risk exists in all competitive business although the balance between financial risks of the type described above and general and management risk varies with the type of business engaged in. The key objective of the risk management function within a financial institution is to allow for a clear understanding of the risks and exposures the firm is engaged in, such that monetary loss is deemed acceptable by the firm. The acceptability of any loss should be on the basis that such (occasional) loss is to be expected as a result of the firm being engaged in a particular business activity. If the bank's risk management function is effective, there will be no over-reaction to any unexpected losses, which may increase eventual costs to many times the original loss amount.

The risk management function

While there is no one agreed organisation structure for the risk management function, the following may be taken as being reflective of the typical bank set-up:

- an independent, 'middle office' department responsible for drawing up and explicitly stating the bank's approach to risk, and defining trading limits and the areas of the market that the firm can have exposure to;

- the head of the risk function reporting to an independent senior manager, who is a member of the executive board;
- monitoring the separation of duties between front, middle and back office, often in conjunction with an internal audit function;
- reporting to senior management, including firm's overall exposure and adherence of the front office to the firm's overall risk strategy;
- communication of risks and risk strategy to shareholders;
- where leading edge systems are in use, employment of the risk management function to generate competitive advantage in the market as well as control.

The risk management function is more likely to deliver effective results when there are clear lines of responsibility and accountability. It is also imperative that the department interacts closely with other areas of the front and back office.

In addition to the above the following are often accepted as ingredients of a risk management framework in an institution engaged in investment banking and trading activity:

- proactive management involvement in risk issues;
- daily overview of risk exposure profile and profit and loss (*p&l*) reports;
- VaR as a common measure of risk exposure, in addition to other measures including 'jump risk' to allow for market corrections;
- defined escalation procedures to deal with rising levels of trading loss, as well as internal 'stop-loss' limits;
- independent daily monitoring of risk utilisation by middle-office risk management function;
- independent production of daily p&l, and independent review of front-office closing prices on a daily basis;
- independent validation of market pricing, and pricing and VaR models.

These guidelines, adopted universally in the investment banking community, should assist in the development of an influential and effective risk management function for all financial institutions.

Managing risk

The different stakeholders in a bank or financial institution will have slightly different perspectives on risk and its management. If we were to generalise, shareholders will wish for stable earnings as well as the highest possible return on capital. From the point of view of business managers though, the perspective may be slightly different and possibly shorter term. For them, risk management often takes the following route:

- create as diversified a set of business lines as possible, and within each business line diversify portfolios to maximum extent;
- establish procedures to enable some measure of forecasting of market prices;
- hedge the portfolio to minimise losses when market forecasts suggest that losses are to be expected.

The VaR measurement tool falls into the second and third areas of this strategy. It is used to give an idea of risk exposure (generally, to market and credit risk only) so that banks can stay within trading limits, and to feed into the hedge calculation.

QUANTITATIVE MEASUREMENT OF RISK

Before introducing the concept of VaR we will consider three standard measures of risk used in the investment community.

Standard deviation

We defined 'risk' above as a prelude to considering its measurement in a VaR context. Investment 'risk' tends to be viewed differently by academics and investors. Academics consider risk within modern portfolio theory to be defined as standard deviation or volatility. To investors risk usually is the probability of loss. Standard deviation is a traditional measure often used by investment professionals. It measures an investment's variability of returns; that is, its volatility in relation to its average return.

While standard deviation has the cachet of science it is a narrow measure and may not provide sufficient information by itself. It is simply a measure of volatility and as a measure of the *probability* of loss is of limited use. However, its usefulness is increased if one pairs

it with returns, as in the Sharpe Ratio or the Van Ratio. Moving on
from here, the concept of VaR is built on obtaining *probabilities* of
loss based on the distribution of returns from a market investment
instrument.

Sharpe Ratio

The Sharpe Ratio is a reward–risk ratio. It measures the extent to
which the return of an investment (above the *risk-free* return)
exceeds its volatility. The higher the ratio, the more reward an
investment provides for the risk incurred. The ratio is calculated
according to the following equation:

$$\text{Sharpe Ratio} = \frac{R_m - R_f}{V_m} \tag{1.1}$$

where R_m = Rate of return of investment m;
         R_f = Risk-free rate of return (e.g., T-Bill);
         V_m = Standard deviation of instrument m.

A ratio of 0.5 is considered fair return for risk incurred. For an
investor it is more useful as a relative measure, in comparing the
ratio of one investment to that of another. For bank trading desks it is
a useful measure of the return generated against the risk incurred, for
which the return and volatility of individual trading books can be
compared with that on the risk-free instrument (or a bank book
trading only T-bills).

Van Ratio

The Van Ratio expresses the probability of an investment suffering a
loss for a defined period, usually 1 year. For example, a Van Ratio of
20% indicates that there is a 1 in 5 chance of a loss during every four-
quarter rolling window. The ratio first uses the following fraction to
calculate this probability:

$$\frac{\text{Compound annual return for the measurement period}}{\text{Average four-quarter standard deviation for the measurement period}} \tag{1.2}$$

The probability of a loss is then calculated using standard normal
curve probability tables.

The Van Ratio provides an intuitive measure of *absolute* risk, the concept of the probability of a loss. To this end its calculation has assumed a normal distribution of returns. The assumption of normality of returns is important in the concept of VaR as calculated by most of the models and methodologies in use in financial institutions.

Chapter

2

VOLATILITY AND
CORRELATION

Value-at-Risk (VaR) is essentially a measure of volatility, specific-ally how volatile a bank's assets are. Assets that exhibit high volatility present higher risk. VaR also takes into account the corre-lation between different sets of assets in the overall portfolio. If the market price performance of assets is closely positively correlated, this also presents higher risk. So, before we begin the discussion of VaR we need to be familiar with these two concepts. Readers who have an investor's understanding of elementary statistics may skip this chapter and move straight to Chapter 3.

STATISTICAL CONCEPTS

The statistics used in VaR calculations are based on well-established concepts. There are standard formulae for calculating the mean and standard deviation of a set of values. If we assume that X is a random variable with particular values x, we can apply the basic formula to calculate mean and standard deviation. Remember that the mean is the average of the set of values or observations, while the standard deviation is a measure of the dispersion away from the mean of the range of values. In fact, the standard deviation is the square root of the variance, but the variance, being the sum of squared deviations of each value from the mean divided by the number of observations, is of little value for us.

Arithmetic mean

We say that the random variable is X, so the mean is $E(X)$. In a time series of observations of historical data, the probability values are the frequencies of the observed values. The mean is:

$$E(X) = \frac{\sum_i x_i}{n} \qquad (2.1)$$

where $1/n =$ Assigned probability to a single value among n; and
          $n =$ Number of observations.

The standard deviation of the set of values is:

$$\sigma(X) = \frac{1}{n}\sqrt{\sum_i [x_i - E(X)]^2} \qquad (2.2)$$

The probability assigned to a set of values is given by the type of distribution and, in fact, from a distribution we can determine mean and standard deviation depending on the probabilities p_i assigned to each value x_i of the random variable X. The sum of all probabilities must be 100%. From probability values then, the mean is given by:

$$E(X) \frac{\sum_i p_i x_i}{n} \tag{2.3}$$

The variance is the average weighted by the probabilities of the squared deviations from the mean; so, of course, the standard deviation – which we now call volatility – is the square root of this value. The volatility is given by:

$$\sigma(X) = \sqrt{\sum_i p_i [x_i - E(X)]^2} \tag{2.4}$$

In the example in Table 2.1 we show the calculation of mean, variance and standard deviation as calculated from an Excel spreadsheet. The expectation is the mean of all the observations, while the variance is, as we noted earlier, the sum of squared deviations from the mean. The standard deviation is the square root of the variance.

What happens when we have observations that can assume any value within a range, rather than the discrete values we have seen in our example? When there is a probability that a variable can have a value

Table 2.1 Calculation of standard deviation.

Dates	Observations	Deviations from mean	Squared deviation
1	22	4.83	23.36
2	15	−2.17	4.69
3	13	−4.17	17.36
4	14	−3.17	10.03
5	16	−1.17	1.36
6	17	−0.17	0.03
7	16	−1.17	1.36
8	19	1.83	3.36
9	21	3.83	14.69
10	20	2.83	8.03
11	17	−0.17	0.03
12	16	−1.17	1.36
Sum	206	Sum	85.66
Mean	17.17	Variance	7.788
		Standard deviation	2.791

of any measure between a range of specified values, we have a continuous distribution.

Probability distributions

A probability distribution is a model for an actual or empirical distribution. If we are engaged in an experiment in which a coin is tossed a number of times, the number of heads recorded will be a discrete value of 0, 1, 2, 3, 4, or so on, depending on the number of times we toss the coin. The result is called a 'discrete' random variable. Of course, we know that the probability of throwing a head is 50%, because there are only two outcomes in a coin-toss experiment, heads or tails. We may throw the coin three times and get three heads (it is unlikely but by no means exceptional); however, performing the experiment a great number of times should produce something approaching our 50% result. So, an experiment with a large number of trials would produce an empirical distribution which would be close to the theoretical distribution as the number of tosses increases.

This example illustrates a discrete set of outcomes (0, 1, 2, 3); in other words, a discrete probability distribution. It is equally possible to have a continuous probability distribution: for example, the probability that the return on a portfolio lies between 3% and 7% is associated with a continuous probability distribution because the final return value can assume any value between those two parameters.

The normal distribution

A very commonly used theoretical distribution is the normal distribution, which is plotted as a bell-shaped curve and is familiar to most practitioners in business. The theoretical distribution actually looks like many observed distributions such as the height of people, shoe sizes, and so on. The distribution is completely described by the mean and standard deviation. The normal distribution $N(\mu, \sigma)$ has mean μ and standard deviation σ. The probability function is given by:

$$P(X = x) = \frac{1}{\sigma\sqrt{2\pi}} \exp\left[-\frac{(x - \mu)^2}{2\sigma^2}\right] \qquad (2.5)$$

The distribution is standardised as $N(0, 1)$ with a mean of 0 and a standard deviation of 1. It is possible to obtain probability values for any part of the distribution by using the standardised curve and converting variables to this standardised distribution; thus, the variable $Z = (X - \mu)/\sigma$ follows the standardised normal distribution $N(0, 1)$ with probability:

$$P(Z = Z) = \frac{1}{\sigma\sqrt{2\pi}} \exp\left[-\frac{Z^2}{2\sigma^2}\right] \qquad (2.6)$$

The *Central Limit Theorem* (known also as the law of large numbers) is the basis for the importance of the normal distribution in statistical theory, and in real life a large number of distributions tend towards the normal, provided that there are a sufficient number of observations. This explains the importance of the normal distribution in statistics. If we have large numbers of observations – for example, the change in stock prices, or closing prices in government bonds – it makes calculations straightforward if we assume that they are normally distributed.

Often, as we have seen in the discussions on VaR, it is convenient to assume that the returns from holding an asset are normally distributed. It is often convenient to define the return in logarithmic form as:

$$\ln\left(\frac{P_t}{P_{t-1}}\right)$$

where P_t = Price today;
                 P_{t-1} = Previous price.

If this is assumed to be normally distributed, then the underlying price will have a log-normal distribution. The log-normal distribution never goes to a negative value, unlike the normal distribution, and hence is intuitively more suitable for asset prices. The distribution is illustrated as Figure 2.1.

The normal distribution is assumed to apply to the returns associated with stock prices, and indeed all financial time series observations. However, it is not strictly accurate, as it implies extreme negative values that are not observed in practice. For this reason the log-normal distribution is used instead, in which case the logarithm of the returns is used instead of the return values themselves; this also removes the probability of negative stock prices. In the log-normal distribution, the logarithm of the random variable follows a normal distribution. The log-normal distribution is asymmetric,

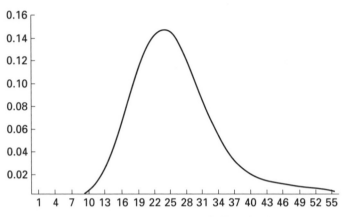

Figure 2.1 The log-normal distribution.

unlike the normal curve, because it does not have negatives at the extreme values.

Confidence intervals

Assume an estimate x of the average of a given statistical population where the true mean of the population is μ. Suppose that we believe that on average $\bar{x}$ is an unbiased estimator of μ. Although this means that on average $\bar{x}$ is accurate, the specific sample that we observe will almost certainly be above or below the true level. Accordingly, if we want to be reasonably confident that our inference is correct, we cannot claim that μ is precisely equal to the observed $\bar{x}$.

Instead, we must construct an interval estimate or confidence interval of the following form:

$$\mu = \bar{x} \pm \text{Sampling error}$$

The crucial question is: How wide must this confidence interval level be? The answer, of course, will depend on how much $\bar{x}$ fluctuates. We first set our requirements for level of confidence; that is, how certain we wish to be statistically. If we wish to be incorrect only 1 day in 20 – that is, we wish to be right 19 days each month (a month is assumed to have 20 working days) – that would equate to a 95% confidence interval that our estimate is accurate. We also assume that our observations are normally distributed. In that case we would expect that the population would be distributed along the lines portrayed in Figure 2.2.

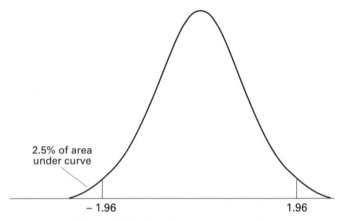

2.5% of area
under curve

−1.96   1.96

Figure 2.2   Confidence intervals.

In the normal distribution, 2.5% of the outcomes are expected to fall more than 1.96 standard deviations from the mean. So, that means 95% of the outcomes would be expected to fall within ±1.96 standard deviations. That is, there is a 95% chance that the random variable will fall between −1.96 standard deviations and +1.96 standard deviations. This would be referred to as a 'two-sided' (or 'two-tailed') confidence interval. It gives the probability of a move upwards or downwards by the random variable outside the limits we are expecting.

In the financial markets, we do not however expect negative prices, so that values below 0 are not really our concern. In this scenario, it makes sense to consider a one-sided test if we are concerned with the risk of loss: a move upward into profit is of less concern (certainly to a risk manager anyway!). From the statistical tables associated with the normal distribution we know that 5% of the outcomes are expected to fall more than 1.645 (rounded to 1.65) standard deviations from the mean. This would be referred to as a one-sided confidence interval.

VOLATILITY

In financial market terms, volatility is a measure of how much the price of an asset moves each day (or week or month, and so on). Speaking generally, higher volatility equates to higher profit or loss. Bankers must be familiar with volatility, as assets that exhibit higher volatility must be priced such that their returns incorporate a 'risk premium' to compensate the holder for the added risk exposure.

Example 2.1

We demonstrate volatility from first principles here. Table 2.2 shows two portfolios, outwardly quite similar. They have virtually identical means from an observation of portfolio return over ten observation periods. However, the standard deviation shows a different picture, and we see that Portfolio B exhibits much greater volatility than Portfolio A. Its future performance is much harder to predict with any reasonable confidence. Portfolio B carries higher risk and so would carry higher VaR. We see also from Table 2.2 that standard deviation is a measure of the dispersion away from the mean of all the observations. To be comfortable that the statistical measures are as accurate as possible, we need the greatest number of observations.

Table 2.2

	B Observations	C Portfolio A (%)	D Portfolio B (%)
6			
7	1	5.08	3.50
8	2	5.00	5.00
9	3	5.05	6.25
10	4	5.00	7.10
11	5	5.05	3.75
12	6	5.00	5.75
13	7	5.01	2.50
14	8	5.20	4.75
15	9	5.06	5.25
16	10	5.00	6.75
17			
18			
19			
20	Mean	5.05	5.06
21	Standard deviation	0.000 622 272	0.014 813 282
22			
23	Excel formula	=AVERAGE(C7:C16)	=AVERAGE(D7:D16)
24		=STDEV(C7:C16)	=STDEV(D7:D16)

The volatility demonstrated above is historical volatility; it is based on past performance. Options traders deal in implied volatility, which is the volatility value given by backing out the Black–Scholes options pricing formula from market prices to obtain an implied volatility value for an asset.

Volatility is important for both VaR measurement and in the valuation of options. It is a method of measuring current asset price against the distribution of the asset's future price. Statistically, volatility is defined as the fluctuation in the underlying asset price over a certain period of time. Fluctuation is derived from the change in price between one day's closing price and the next day's closing price. Where the asset price is stable it will exhibit low volatility, and the opposite when price movements are large and/or unstable.

We saw from Table 2.2 that the average values for low- and high-volatility portfolios were similar; however, the distribution of the recordings differ. The low-volatility portfolio showed low variability in the distribution. High-volatility assets show a wider variability around the mean.

Market practitioners wish to obtain a volatility value that approximates around the normal distribution. This is done by recording a sufficiently large volume of data and reducing the price change intervals to as small an amount as possible; this means that the price changes can be described statistically by the normal distribution curve. We saw earlier in the chapter that the normal distribution curve has two numerical properties known as mean and standard deviation. The mean is the average reading taken at the centre of the curve, and the standard deviation is a value which represents the dispersion around the mean. We demonstrate some examples at Figures 2.3 and 2.4.

In Figure 2.5, standard deviation is shown correlated with dispersion. The curve can be divided into segments which represent specific percentages within each band.

We see from Figure 2.5 that 68.3% of data fall within ±1 standard deviation, 95.5% of data fall within ±2 standard deviations and 99.7% fall within ±3 standard deviations.

The normal distribution curve can also be used to predict future daily share fluctuation over a measured period of time. Future

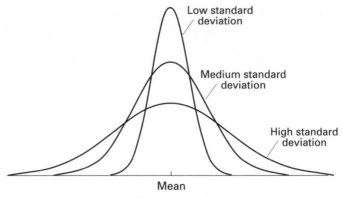

Figure 2.3 Differing standard deviations.

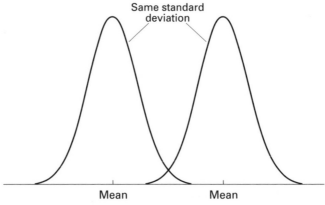

Figure 2.4 Differing means around the same standard deviation.

price distribution uses the volatility expressed as a 1 standard deviation price change at the end of 1 year.

This can be expressed as a percentage:

1 standard deviation price change (p) = Volatility (%)

$\times$ Current asset price (p)

Although the value of an option relies upon estimated future volatility, volatility is shown also as historical volatility and implied volatility. *Historical volatility* is the actual price fluctuation in a given time period. The value will depend on the length of the observation period and when the value was observed. This naturally

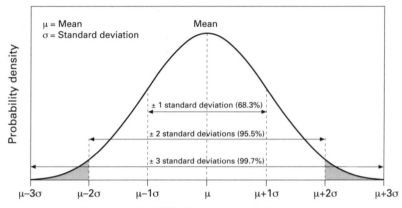

Figure 2.5 Differing standard deviations.

smoothes out day-to- day fluctuations, a moving average of historical volatility can be shown graphically in a similar way as conventional share prices. Figure 2.6 shows a 5-day historical volatility chart reversing through a specified time period.

Although historical volatility can show trends over a greater period of time – for example, 4 years – it can also make distinctly significant and highly variable changes. Therefore, there can be no certainty that a past trend is in any way indicative of a share's future performance.

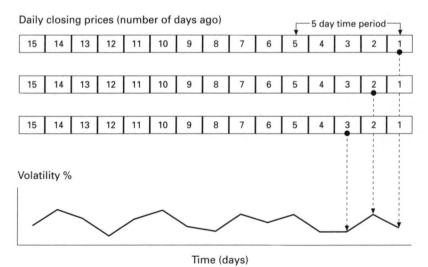

Figure 2.6 Historical volatility chart.

Implied volatility is a necessary tool to obtain the predicted value of an option which has been obtained from the present value of that option by entering different levels of volatility into an option pricing model, until the current market price is reached. This iterative process effectively reduces the margin of error. In a working situation, most option pricing models allow the calculation of implied volatility by entering the present market price for an option.

Future volatility is the predicted or expected price fluctuation of a period of time until the option has expired. Evidently, this will be affected not only by the calculated implied volatility but also by the expectation of the share's price trend.

THE NORMAL DISTRIBUTION AND VaR

As we will see from Chapter 3 there is more than one way to calculate VaR for an asset portfolio. Many VaR models use the normal curve to calculate the estimation of losses over a specified time period. Normal distribution curve tables, which can be looked up in any number of statistics textbooks or on the Internet, show the probability of an observation moving a specific distance away from the recorded mean. Some specific probabilities are given in Table 2.3.

Table 2.3 shows that 95% of all observations in a normal distribution lie within +1.65 standard deviations of the mean. A 95% percentile is often used in VaR calculations. Let us take this further. Consider a gilt portfolio of £20 million with a mean return of 5% per annum. If the standard deviation of the returns is 1.63 what probability is there that returns will fall to 4% within the holding period of 1 year? We require the area of the normal curve at which the 4% value is marked – that is, 27% of the area to the left of the mean. The results are shown at Table 2.4, which also shows the Excel formula.

We should note that, although the markets assume a normal distribution of asset (equity and bond) prices, from observation we know that prices follow a more skewed distribution. In practice, asset prices exhibit what is known as 'leptokurtosis', also known as 'fat tails', which is a normal distribution with fatter tails than the theoretical. In other words, extreme price movements such as stock market corrections occur more frequently than the normal distribution would suggest.

Table 2.3 Probabilities extracted from the normal distribution table.

		E	F	G	H	I	J
		E	*F*	*G*	*H*	*I*	
8	No. of standard deviations	-1.645	-1.000	0.000	1.000	1.650	2.450
9	Probability	5.00%	15.87%	50.00%	84.13%	95.05%	99.29%
10	Excel formula	=NORMSDIST(E8)					

Table 2.4 Normal distribution illustrated for portfolio return.

	C	*D*	*E*	*F*	*G*	*H*	*I*
6							
7	Observation	1	2	3	4	5	6
8	Mean return	5%	5%	5%	5%	5%	5%
9	Target return	4%	5%	6%	7%	8%	8%
10	Standard deviation of return	1.63%	1.63%	1.63%	1.63%	1.63%	1.63%
11	Number of standard deviations	-0.612369871	0	0.612369871	1.224739743	1.837109614	1.837109614
12	Probability	27.01%	50.00%	72.99%	88.97%	96.69%	96.69%

Excel formula
Number of standard deviations = (D9-D8)/D10
Probability = NORMSDIST(D11)

Options traders need to correct for this more than others. The standard option pricing model, the Black–Scholes Formula, which we look at in Chapter 5, uses the normal distribution to calculate the delta of the option – the $N(d1)$ part of the formula – and the probability that the option will be exercised, the $N(d2)$ part. In practice, the implied volatility of an option is higher if it is deeply in-the-money or out-of-the-money. This is known as the option 'smile', and reflects market understanding that the normal distribution is not a completely accurate description of market price behaviour.

CORRELATION

The correlation between different assets and classes of assets is an important measure for risk managers because of the role diversification plays in risk reduction. Correlation is a measure of how much the price of one asset moves in relation to the price of another asset. In a portfolio comprised of only two assets, the VaR of this portfolio is reduced if the correlation between the two assets is weak or negative.

The simplest measure of correlation is the correlation coefficient. This is a value between -1 and $+1$, with a perfect positive correlation indicated by 1, while a perfect negative correlation is given by -1. Note that this assumes a linear (straight line) relationship between the two assets. A correlation of 0 suggests that there is no linear relationship.

We illustrate these values at Table 2.5, which is a hypothetical set of observations showing the volatilities of four different government benchmark bonds. Note also the Excel formula so that readers can reproduce their own analyses. We assume these bonds are different sovereign names. Bonds 1, 3 and 4 have very similar average returns, but the relationship between Bond 3 and Bond 1 is negatively closely correlated, whereas Bond 4 is positively closely correlated with Bond 1. Bond 2 has a very low positive correlation with Bond 1, and we conclude that there is very little relationship in the price movement of these two bonds.

What are we to make of these four different sovereign names with regard to portfolio diversification? On first glance, Bonds 1 and 3 would appear to offer perfect diversification because they are strongly negatively correlated. However, calculating a diversified

Table 2.5 Correlation.

Cell	C	D	E	F	G
	Observation	Government bond 1	Government bond 2	Government bond 3	Government bond 4
5					
6	1	5.35%	11.00%	7.15%	5.20%
7	2	6.00%	9.00%	7.30%	6.00%
8	3	5.50%	9.60%	6.90%	5.80%
9	4	6.00%	13.70%	7.20%	6.30%
10	5	5.90%	12.00%	5.90%	5.90%
11	6	6.50%	10.80%	6.00%	6.05%
12	7	7.15%	10.10%	6.10%	7.00%
13	8	6.80%	12.40%	5.60%	6.80%
14	9	6.75%	14.70%	5.40%	6.70%
15	10	7.00%	13.50%	5.45%	7.20%
16					
17					
18	Mean return	6.30%	11.68%	6.30%	6.30%
19	Volatility	0.00631	0.01897	0.00760	0.00622
20	Correlation with bond 1		0.357617936	−0.758492885	0.933620205
21					
22	**Excel formula**				
23	Mean return	= AVERAGE(E6:E15)			
24	Volatility	= STDEV(E6:E15)			
25	Correlation with bond 1	= CORREL(E6:E15,D6:D15)			

VaR for such a portfolio would underestimate risk exposure in times of market correction – which is, after all, when managers most want to know what their risk is. This is because, even though the bonds are negatively related, they can both be expected to fall in value when the market overall is dropping. Bond 2 is no good for risk mitigation, it is strongly positively correlated. Bond 2 has essentially no relationship with Bond 1; however, it is also the most risky security in the portfolio.

We will apply what we have learned here in Chapter 3.

Chapter

3

· ·

VALUE-AT-RISK

The advent of value-at-risk (*VaR*) as an accepted methodology for quantifying market risk and its adoption by bank regulators are milestones in the evolution of risk management. The application of VaR has been extended from its initial use in securities houses to commercial banks and corporates, following its introduction in October 1994 when JP Morgan launched RiskMetrics free over the Internet.

In this chapter we look at the different methodologies employed to calculate VaR, and also illustrate its application to simple portfolios. We look first at the variance–covariance method, which is arguably the most popular estimation technique.

WHAT IS VaR?

VaR is an estimate of an amount of money. It is based on probabilities, so cannot be relied on with certainty, but is rather a level of confidence which is selected by the user in advance. VaR measures the volatility of a company's assets, and so the greater the volatility, the higher the probability of loss.

Definition

Essentially VaR is a measure of the volatility of a bank trading book. It is the characteristics of volatility that traders, risk managers and others wish to become acquainted with when assessing a bank's risk exposure. The mathematics behind measuring and estimating volatility is a complex business, and we do not go into it here. However, by making use of a volatility estimate, a trader or senior manager can gain some idea of the risk exposure of the trading book, using the VaR measure.

VaR is defined as follows:

> **VaR is a measure of market risk. It is the maximum loss which can occur with $X\%$ confidence over a holding period of t days.**

VaR is the expected loss of a portfolio over a specified time period for a set level of probability. So, for example, if a daily VaR is stated as £100,000 to a 95% level of confidence, this means that during the day there is a only a 5% chance that the loss will be *greater* than £100,000. VaR measures the potential loss in market value of a portfolio using estimated volatility and correlations. It is measured within a given confidence interval, typically 95% or 99%. The concept seeks to measure the possible losses from a position or portfolio under 'normal' circumstances. The definition of normality is critical to the estimation of VaR and is a statistical concept; its importance varies according to the VaR calculation methodology that is being used.

Broadly speaking, the calculation of a VaR estimate follows four steps:

1. *Determine the time horizon over which the firm wishes to estimate a potential loss* – this horizon is set by the user. In practice, time horizons of 1 day to 1 year have been used. For instance, bank front-office traders are often interested in calculating the amount they might lose in a 1-day period. Regulators and participants in illiquid markets may want to estimate exposures to market risk over a longer period. In any case a time horizon must be specified by the decision-maker.

2. *Select the degree of certainty required, which is the confidence level that applies to the VaR estimate* – knowing the largest likely loss a bank will suffer 95 times out of 100, or in fact on 1 day out of 20 (i.e., a 95% degree of confidence in this estimate, or confidence interval) may be sufficient. For regulatory requirements a 99% confidence interval may be more appropriate. Senior management and shareholders are often interested in the potential loss arising from catastrophe situations, such as a stock market crash, so for them a 99% confidence level is more appropriate.

3. *Create a probability distribution of likely returns for the instrument or portfolio under consideration* – several methods may be used. The easiest to understand is a distribution of recent historical returns for the asset or portfolio which often looks like the curve associated with the normal distribution. After determining a time horizon and confidence interval for the estimate, and then collating the history of market price changes in a probability distribution, we can apply the laws of statistics to estimate VaR.

4. *Calculate the VaR estimate* – this is done by observing the loss amount associated with that area beneath the normal curve at the critical confidence interval value that is statistically associated with the probability chosen for the VaR estimate in Step 2.

These four steps will in theory allow us to calculate a VaR estimate 'longhand', although in practice mathematical models exist that will do this for us. Bearing these steps in mind, we can arrive at a practical definition of VaR not much removed from our first one:

> **VaR is the largest likely loss from market risk (expressed in currency units) that an asset or portfolio will suffer over a time interval and with a degree of certainty selected by the user.**

There are a number of methods for calculating VaR, all logically sustainable, and estimates prepared using the different methodologies can vary dramatically. At this point it is worthwhile reminding ourselves what VaR is *not*. It is not a unified method for measuring risk, as the different calculation methodologies each produce different VaR values. In addition, as it is a quantitative statistical technique, VaR only captures risks that can be quantified. Therefore, it does not measure (and nor does it seek to measure) other risks that a bank or securities house will be exposed to, such as liquidity risk or operational risk. Most importantly, VaR is not 'risk management'. This term refers to the complete range of duties and disciplines that are involved in minimising and managing bank risk exposure. VaR is but one ingredient of risk management, a measurement tool for market risk.

METHODOLOGY

Centralised database

To implement VaR, all of a firm's positions data must be gathered into one centralised database. Once this is complete the overall risk has to be calculated by aggregating the risks from individual instruments across the entire portfolio. The potential move in each instrument (i.e., each risk factor) has to be inferred from past daily price movements over a given observation period. For regulatory purposes this period is at least 1 year. Hence, the data on which VaR estimates are based should capture all relevant daily market moves over the previous year. The main assumption underpinning VaR – and which in turn may be seen as its major weakness – is that the distribution of future price and rate changes will follow past variations. Therefore, the potential portfolio loss calculations for VaR are worked out using distributions from historic price data in the observation period.

Correlation assumptions

VaR requires that the user decide which exposures are allowed to offset each other and by how much. For example, is the Japanese yen correlated to movements in the euro or the Mexican peso? Consider also the price of crude oil to movements in the price of natural gas: if there is a correlation, to what extent is the degree of correlation? VaR requires that the user determine correlations *within* markets as well as *across* markets. The mapping procedures used as part of the VaR process also have embedded correlation assumptions. For example, mapping individual stocks into the S&P 500 or fixed interest securities into the swap curve translate into the assumption that individual financial instruments move as the market overall. This is reasonable for diversified portfolios but may fall down for undiversified or illiquid portfolios.

To calculate the VaR for a single security, we would calculate the standard deviation of its price returns. This can be done using historical data, but more commonly using the *implied volatility* contained in exchange-traded option prices. We would then select a confidence interval and apply this to the standard deviation, which would be our VaR measure. This is considered in more detail later.

There are three main methods for calculating VaR. As with all statistical models, they depend on certain assumptions. They are:

- the correlation method (or variance/covariance method);
- historical simulation;
- Monte Carlo simulation.

Correlation method

This is also known as the variance–covariance, parametric or analytic method. This method assumes the returns on risk factors are normally distributed, the correlations between risk factors are constant and the delta (or price sensitivity to changes in a risk factor) of each portfolio constituent is constant. Using the correlation method, the volatility of each risk factor is extracted from the historical observation period. Historical data on investment returns are therefore required. The potential effect of each component of the portfolio on the overall portfolio value is then worked out from the component's delta (with respect to a particular risk factor) and that risk factor's volatility.

There are different methods of calculating the relevant risk factor volatilities and correlations. We consider two alternatives:

(i) Simple *historic volatility* (correlation) – this is the most straightforward method but the effects of a large one-off market move can significantly distort volatilities (correlations) over the required forecasting period. For example, if using 30-day historic volatility, a market shock will stay in the volatility figure for 30 days until it drops out of the sample range and, correspondingly, causes a sharp drop in (historic) volatility 30 days *after* the event. This is because each past observation is equally weighted in the volatility calculation.

(ii) A more sophisticated approach is to weight past observations unequally. This is done to give more weight to recent observations so that large jumps in volatility are not caused by events that occurred some time ago. Two methods for unequal weighting are the generalised autoregressive conditional heteroscedasticity (*GARCH*) models and exponentially weighted moving averages. GARCH models are fine-tuned to each risk factor time series, while exponentially weighted averages can be computed with little more complication than simple historic volatility. Both methods rely on the assumption that future volatilities can be predicted from historic price movements.

Historical simulation method

The historical simulation method for calculating VaR is the simplest and avoids some of the pitfalls of the correlation method. Specifically, the three main assumptions behind correlation (normally distributed returns, constant correlations, constant deltas) are not needed in this case. For historical simulation the model calculates potential losses using actual historical returns in the risk factors and so captures the non-normal distribution of risk factor returns. This means rare events and crashes can be included in the results. As the risk factor returns used for revaluing the portfolio are actual past movements, the correlations in the calculation are also actual past correlations. They capture the dynamic nature of correlation as well as scenarios when the usual correlation relationships break down.

Monte Carlo simulation method

The third method, Monte Carlo simulation is more flexible than the previous two. As with historical simulation, Monte Carlo simulation allows the risk manager to use actual historical distributions for risk factor returns rather than having to assume normal returns. A large number of randomly generated simulations are run forward in time using volatility and correlation estimates chosen by the risk manager. Each simulation will be different, but in total the simulations will aggregate to the chosen statistical parameters (i.e., historical distributions and volatility and correlation estimates). This method is more realistic than the previous two models and, therefore, is more likely to estimate VaR more accurately. However, its implementation requires powerful computers and there is also a trade-off in that the time to perform calculations is longer.

Validity of the volatility-correlation VaR estimate

The level of confidence in the VaR estimation process is selected by the number of standard deviations of variance applied to the probability distribution. A standard deviation selection of 1.645 provides a 95% confidence level (in a one-tailed test) that the potential estimated price movement will not be more than a given amount based on the correlation of market factors to the position's price sensitivity. This confidence level is advocated by the RiskMetrics version of volatility-correlation VaR.

HOW TO CALCULATE VALUE-AT-RISK

A conceptual illustration of the normal distribution being applied for VaR is given at Figure 3.1.

A market risk estimate can be calculated by following these steps:

1. Value the current portfolio using today's prices, the components of which are 'market factors'. For example, the market factors that affect the value of a bond denominated in a foreign currency are the term structure of that currency's interest rate (either the zero-coupon curve or the par yield curve) and the exchange rate.

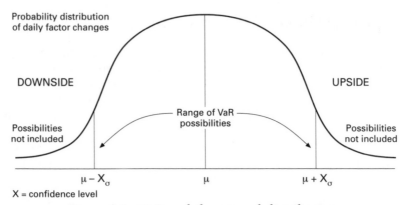

Probability distribution
of daily factor changes

DOWNSIDE   UPSIDE

────── Range of VaR ──────
possibilities

Possibilities   Possibilities
not included   not included

$\mu - X_\sigma$ μ $\mu + X_\sigma$

X = confidence level

Figure 3.1 VaR and the normal distribution.

2. Revalue the portfolio using alternative prices based on changed market factors and calculate the change in the portfolio value that would result.
3. Revaluing the portfolio using a number of alternative prices gives a distribution of changes in value. Given this, a portfolio VaR can be specified in terms of confidence levels.
4. The risk manager can calculate the maximum the firm can lose over a specified time horizon at a specified probability level.

In implementing VaR the main problem is finding a way to obtain a series of vectors of different market factors. We will see how the various methodologies try to resolve this issue for each of the three methods that can be used to calculate VaR.

Historical method

Values of the market factors for a particular historical period are collected and changes in these values over the time horizon are observed for use in the calculation. For instance, if a 1-day VaR is required using the past 100 trading days, each of the market factors will have a vector of observed changes that will be made up of the 99 changes in value of the market factor. A vector of alternative values is created for each of the market factors by adding the current value of the market factor to each of the values in the vector of observed changes.

The portfolio value is found using the current and alternative values for the market factors. The changes in portfolio value between the current value and the alternative values are then calculated. The final step is to sort the changes in portfolio value from the lowest value to highest value and determine VaR based on the desired confidence interval. For a 1-day, 95% confidence level VaR using the past 100 trading days, the VaR would be the 95th most adverse change in portfolio value.

Simulation method

The first step is to define the parameters of the distributions for the changes in market factors, including correlations among these factors. Normal and log-normal distributions are usually used to estimate changes in market factors, while historical data are most often used to define correlations among market factors. The distributions are then used in a Monte Carlo simulation to obtain simulated changes in the market factors over the time horizon to be used in the VaR calculation.

A vector of alternative values is created for each of the market factors by adding the current value of the market factor to each of the values in the vector of simulated changes. Once this vector of alternative values of the market factors is obtained, the current and alternative values for the portfolio, the changes in portfolio value and the VaR are calculated exactly as in the historical method.

Variance–covariance, analytic or parametric method

This is similar to the historical method in that historical values of market factors are collected in a database. The next steps are then to:

(i) decompose the instruments in the portfolio into the cash-equivalent positions in more basic instruments;
(ii) specify the exact distributions for the market factors (or 'returns'); and
(iii) calculate portfolio variance and VaR using standard statistical methods.

We now look at these steps in greater detail.

Decompose financial instruments

The analytic method assumes that financial instruments can be decomposed or 'mapped' into a set of simpler instruments that are exposed to only one market factor. For example, a 2-year UK gilt can be mapped into a set of zero-coupon bonds representing each cash flow. Each of these zero-coupon bonds is exposed to only one market factor – a specific UK zero-coupon interest rate. Similarly, a foreign currency bond can be mapped into a set of zero-coupon bonds and a cash foreign exchange amount subject to movement in the spot foreign exchange (FX) rate.

Specify distributions

The analytic method makes assumptions about the distributions of market factors. For example, the most widely used analytic method, JP Morgan's RiskMetrics, assumes that the underlying distributions are normal. With normal distributions all the historical information is summarised in the mean, variance and covariance of the returns (market factors), so users do not need to keep all the historical data.

Calculate portfolio variance and VaR

If all the market factors are assumed to be normally distributed, the portfolio, which is the sum of the individual instruments, can also be assumed to be normally distributed. This means that the portfolio variance can be calculated using standard statistical methods (similar to modern portfolio theory), namely:

$$\sigma_\rho = \sqrt{\alpha_j^2 \sigma_j^2 + \alpha_k^2 \sigma_k^2 + 2\alpha_j \alpha_k \rho_{jk} \sigma_j \sigma_k} \qquad (3.1)$$

where α_j = Home-currency present value of the position in market factor j;
         σ_j^2 = Variance of market factor j;
         ρ_{jk} = Correlation coefficient between market factors j and k.

The portfolio VaR is then a selected number of portfolio standard deviations; for example, 1.645 standard deviations will isolate 5% of the area of the distribution in the lower tail of the normal curve, providing 95% confidence in the estimate. Consider an example where, using historical data, the portfolio variance for a package of UK gilts is £348.57. The standard deviation of the portfolio would be $\sqrt{348.57}$, which is £18.67. A 95% 1-day VaR would be 1.645 × £18.67, which is £30.71.

Of course, a bank's trading book will contain many hundreds of different assets, and the method employed above, useful for a two-asset portfolio, will become unwieldy. Therefore, matrices are used to calculate the VaR of a portfolio where many correlation coefficients are used. This is considered below.

Matrix calculation of variance–covariance VaR

Consider the following hypothetical portfolio of £10,000,000.00 invested in two assets, as shown in Table 3.1(i). The standard deviation of each asset has been calculated on historical observation of asset returns. Note that *returns* are returns of asset prices, rather than the prices themselves; they are calculated from the actual prices by taking the ratio of closing prices. The returns are then calculated as the logarithm of the price relatives. The mean and standard

Table 3.1(i) Two-asset portfolio VaR.

D	E	F	G	H
		Asset		
8		Bond 1	Bond 2	
9	Standard deviation	11.83%	17.65%	
10	Portfolio weighting	60%	40%	
11	Correlation coefficient			0.647
12	Portfolio value			£10,000,000.00
13	Confidence level			95%
14				
15	Portfolio variance			0.016506998
16	Standard deviation			12.848%
17				
18	95% c.i. standard deviations			1.644853627
19				
20	Value-at-Risk			0.211330072
21	Value-at-Risk £			£2,113,300.72
22				
23				
24				
25				
26				

Table 3.1(ii)   Spreadsheet formulae for Table 3.1(i).

D	E	F	G	H
		Asset		
8		Bond 1	Bond 2	
9	Standard deviation	11.83%	17.65%	
10	Portfolio weighting	60%	40%	
11	Correlation coefficient			0.647
12	Portfolio value			£10,000,000.00
13	Confidence level			95%
14				
15	Portfolio variance		=F9^2*F10^2+G9^2*G10^2+2*F9*F10*G9*G10	
16	Standard deviation		=H15^0.5	
17				
18	95% c.i. standard deviations		=NORMSINV(H13)	
19				
20	Value-at-Risk		=H18*H16	
21	Value-at-Risk £		=H20*H12	
22				
23				

deviation of the returns are then calculated using standard statistical formulae. This would then give the standard deviation of daily price relatives, which is converted to an annual figure by multiplying it by the square root of the number of days in a year, usually taken to be 250.

We wish to calculate the portfolio VaR at the 95% level. The Excel formulae are shown at Table 3.1(ii).

The standard equation is used to calculate the variance of the portfolio, using the individual asset standard deviations and the asset weightings; the VaR of the book is the square root of the variance. Multiplying this figure by the current value of the portfolio gives us the portfolio VaR, which is £2,113,300.72.

Using historical volatility means that we must define the horizon of the time period of observations, as well as the frequency of observations. Typically, a daily measure is used due to the ease of collating information, with the result that we need to use the 'square root of time' rule when moving to another time period. This applies when there are no bounds to returns data. This was illustrated above when we referred to the square root for the number of working days in a year. As an example, assume a 2% daily volatility, the

1-year volatility then becomes:

$$\sigma_{1\ year} = \sigma_{1\ day}\sqrt{250}$$
$$= 2\% \times 15.811$$
$$= 31.622\%$$

Using this rule we can convert values for market volatility over any period of time.

The RiskMetrics VaR methodology uses matrices to obtain the same results that we have shown here. This is because, once a portfolio starts to contain many assets, the method we described above becomes unwieldy. Matrices allow us to calculate VaR for a portfolio containing many hundreds of assets, which would require assessment of the volatility of each asset and correlations of each asset to all the others in the portfolio. We can demonstrate how the parametric methodology uses variance and correlation matrices to calculate the variance, and hence standard deviation, of a portfolio. The matrices are shown at Figure 3.2. Note that multiplication of matrices carries with it some unique rules; readers who are unfamiliar with matrices should refer to a standard mathematics text.

	Variance matrix		**Correlation matrix**		**VC matrix**	
			Bond 1	Bond 2		
Bond 1	11.83%	0	1	0.647	0.1183	0.076 54
Bond 2	0	17.65%	0.647	1	0.114 196	0.1765

VC matrix		**Variance matrix**		**VCV matrix**	
0.1183	0.076 54	11.83%	0	0.013 995	0.013 509
0.114 196	0.1765	0	17.65%	0.013 509	0.031 152

Weighting matrix		**VCV matrix**		**WVCV**	
60%	40%	0.013 995	0.013 509	0.013 801	0.020 566
		0.013 509	0.031 152		

WVCV		**W**	**WVCVW**
0.013 801	0.020 566	60%	0.016 507
		40%	

| | Standard deviation | 0.128 48 |

Figure 3.2 Matrix variance–covariance calculation for the two-asset portfolio shown in Table 3.1.

As shown at Figure 3.2, using the same two-asset portfolio described, we can set a 2×2 matrix with the individual standard deviations inside; this is labelled the 'variance' matrix. The standard deviations are placed on the horizontal axis of the matrix, and a 0 entered in the other cells. The second matrix is the correlation matrix, and the correlation of the two assets is placed in cells corresponding to the other asset; that is why a '1' is placed in the other cells, as an asset is said to have a correlation of 1 with itself. The two matrices are then multiplied to produce another matrix, labelled 'VC' in Figure 3.2.[1]

The VC matrix is then multiplied by the V matrix to obtain the variance–covariance matrix or VCV matrix. This shows the variance of each asset; for Bond 1 this is 0.013 99, which is expected as that is the square of its standard deviation, which we were given at the start. The matrix also tells us that Bond 1 has a covariance of 0.0135 with Bond 2. We then set up a matrix of the portfolio weighting of the two assets, and this is multiplied by the VCV matrix. This produces a 1×2 matrix, which we need to change to a single number; so, this is multiplied by the W matrix, reset as a 2×1 matrix, which produces the portfolio variance. This is 0.016 507. The standard deviation is the square root of the variance, and is 0.128 4795 or 12.848%, which is what we obtained before. In our illustration it is important to note the order in which the matrices were multiplied, as this will obviously affect the result. The volatility matrix contains the standard deviations along the diagonal, and 0s are entered in all the other cells. So, if the portfolio we were calculating has 50 assets in it, we would require a 50×50 matrix and enter the standard deviations for each asset along the diagonal line. All the other cells would have a 0 in them. Similarly, for the weighting matrix this is always one row, and all the weights are entered along the row. To take the example just given the result would be a 1×50 weighting matrix.

The correlation matrix in the simple example above is set up as shown in Table 3.2.

The correlation matrix at Table 3.2 shows that Asset 1 has a correlation of 0.647 with Asset 2. All correlation tables always have unity

---

[1] A spreadsheet calculator such as Microsoft Excel has a function for multiplying matrices which may be used for any type of matrix. The function is '=MMULT()' typed in all the cells of the product matrix.

Table 3.2   Asset correlation.

	Asset 1	Asset 2
Asset 1	1	0.647
Asset 2	0.647	1

along the diagonal because an asset will have a correlation of 1 with itself. So, a three-asset portfolio of the following correlations

Correlation 1, 2	0.647
Correlation 1, 3	0.455
Correlation 2, 3	0.723

would look like Table 3.3.

The matrix method for calculating the standard deviation is more effective than the first method we described, because it can be used for a portfolio containing a large number of assets. In fact, this is exactly the methodology used by RiskMetrics, and the computer model used for the calculation will be set up with matrices containing the data for hundreds, if not thousands, of different assets.

The variance–covariance method captures the diversification benefits of a multi-product portfolio because the correlation coefficient matrix is used in the calculation. For instance, if the two bonds in our hypothetical portfolio had a negative correlation the VaR number produced would be lower. It was also the first methodology introduced by JP Morgan in 1994. To apply it, a bank would require data on volatility and correlation for the assets in its portfolio. These data are actually available from the RiskMetrics website (and other sources), so a bank does not necessarily need its own data. It may wish to use its own datasets, however, should it have them, to tailor the application to its own use. The advantages of the variance–covariance

Table 3.3   Correlation matrix: three-asset portfolio.

	Asset 1	Asset 2	Asset 3
Asset 1	1	0.647	0.455
Asset 2	0.647	1	0.723
Asset 3	0.455	0.723	1

methodology are that:

- it is simple to apply and fairly straightforward to explain;
- datasets for its use are immediately available.

The drawbacks of the variance–covariance method are that it assumes stable correlations and measures only linear risk; it also places excessive reliance on the normal distribution, and returns in the market are widely believed to have 'fatter tails' than a true to normal distribution. This phenomenon is known as *leptokurtosis*; that is, the non-normal distribution of outcomes. Another disadvantage is that the process requires mapping. To construct a weighting portfolio for the RiskMetrics tool, cash flows from financial instruments are mapped into precise maturity points, known as *grid points*. We will review this later in the chapter; however, in most cases assets do not fit into neat grid points, and complex instruments cannot be broken down accurately into cash flows. The mapping process makes assumptions that frequently do not hold in practice.

Nevertheless, the variance–covariance method is still popular in the market, and is frequently the first VaR method installed at a bank.

Mapping

The cornerstone of variance–covariance methodologies, such as RiskMetrics, is the requirement for data on volatilities and correlations for assets in the portfolio. The RiskMetrics dataset does not contain volatilities for every maturity possible, as that would require a value for every period from 1 day to over 10,950 days (30 years) and longer, and correlations between each of these days. This would result in an excessive amount of calculation. Rather, volatilities are available for set maturity periods (these are shown in Table 3.4).

Table 3.4 RiskMetrics grid points.

1 month	5 years
3 months	7 years
6 months	9 years
1 year	10 years
2 years	15 years
3 years	20 years
4 years	30 years

If a bond is maturing in 6 years' time, its redemption cash flow will not match the data in the RiskMetrics dataset, so it must be mapped to two periods, in this case being split to the 5-year and 7-year grid point. This is done in proportions so that the original value of the bond is maintained once it has been mapped. More importantly, when a cash flow is mapped, it must split in a manner that preserves the volatility characteristic of the original cash flow. Therefore, when mapping cash flows, if one cash flow is apportioned to two grid points, the share of the two new cash flows must equal the present value of the original cash flows, and the combined volatility of the two new assets must be equal to that of the original asset. A simple demonstration is given at Example 3.1.

Example 3.1   Cash flow mapping.

A bond trading book holds £1 million nominal of a gilt strip that is due to mature in precisely 6 years' time. To correctly capture the volatility of this position in the bank's RiskMetrics VaR estimate, the cash flow represented by this bond must be mapped to the grid points for 5 years and 7 years, the closest maturity buckets that the RiskMetrics dataset holds volatility and correlation data for. The present value of the strip is calculated using the 6-year zero-coupon rate, which RiskMetrics obtains by interpolating between the 5-year rate and the 7-year rate. The details are shown in Table 3.5.

Table 3.5   Bond position to be mapped to grid points.

Gilt strip nominal (£)	1,000,000
Maturity (years)	6
5-year zero-coupon rate	5.35%
7-year zero-coupon rate	5.50%
5-year volatility	24.50%
7-year volatility	28.95%
Correlation coefficient	0.979
Lower period	5
Upper period	7

Note that the correlation between the two interest rates is very close to 1; this is expected because 5-year interest rates generally move very closely in line with 7-year rates.

We wish to assign the single cash flow to the 5-year and 7-year grid points (also referred to as *vertices*). The present value of the bond, using the 6-year interpolated yield, is £728,347. This is shown in Table 3.6, which also uses an interpolated volatility to calculate the volatility of the 6-year cash flow. However, we wish to calculate a portfolio volatility based on the apportionment of the cash flow to the 5-year and 7-year grid points. To do this, we need a weighting to use to allocate the cash flow between the two vertices. In the hypothetical situation used here, this presents no problem because 6 years falls precisely between 5 years and 7 years. Therefore, the weightings are 0.5 for Year 5 and 0.5 for Year 7. If the cash flow had fallen in less obvious a maturity point, we would have to calculate the weightings using the formula for portfolio variance.

Using these weightings, we calculate the variance for the new 'portfolio', containing the two new cash flows, and then the standard deviation for the portfolio. This gives us a VaR for the strip of £265,853.

Table 3.6   Cash flow mapping and portfolio variance.

Interpolated yield	0.054 25
Interpolated volatility	0.267 25
Present value	728,347.0103
Weighting 5-year grid point	0.5
Weighting 7-year grid point	0.5
Variance of portfolio	0.070 677 824
Standard deviation	0.265 853 012
VaR (£)	265,853

Confidence intervals

Many models estimate VaR at a given confidence interval, under normal market conditions. This assumes that market returns generally follow a random pattern but one that approximates over time to a normal distribution. The level of confidence at which the VaR is calculated will depend on the nature of the trading book's activity and what the VaR number is being used for. The market risk amendment to the Basel Capital Accord stipulates a 99% confidence interval and a 10-day holding period if the VaR measure is to be used to calculate the regulatory capital requirement. However, certain banks prefer to use other confidence levels and holding periods; the decision on which level to use is a function of asset types in the portfolio, quality of market data available and the accuracy of the model itself, which will have been tested over time by the bank.

For example, a bank may view a 99% confidence interval as providing no useful information, as it implies that there should only be two or three breaches of the VaR measure over the course of 1 year; that would leave no opportunity to test the accuracy of the model until a relatively long period of time had elapsed, in the meantime the bank would be unaware if the model was generating inaccurate numbers. A 95% confidence level implies the VaR level being exceeded around 1 day each month, if a year is assumed to contain 250 days. If a VaR calculation is made using 95% confidence, and a 99% confidence level is required for, say, regulatory purposes, we need to adjust the measure to take account of the change in standard deviations required. For example, a 99% confidence interval corresponds to 2.32 standard deviations, while a 95% level is equivalent to 1.645 standard deviations. Thus, to convert from 95% confidence to 99% confidence, the VaR figure is divided by 1.645 and multiplied by 2.32.

In the same way there may be occasions when a firm will wish to calculate VaR over a different holding period from that recommended by the Basel Committee. The holding period of a portfolio's VaR calculation should represent the period of time required to unwind the portfolio; that is, sell off the assets on the book. A 10-day holding period is recommended but would be unnecessary for a highly liquid portfolio; for example, a market-making book holding government bonds.

To adjust the VaR number to fit it to a new holding period we simply scale it upwards or downwards by the square root of the time period required. For example, a VaR calculation measured for a 10-day holding period will be $\sqrt{10}$ times larger than the corresponding 1-day measure.

COMPARISON BETWEEN METHODS

The three methods produce different VaR estimates and these are more marked with portfolios that contain options. The analytic method usually estimates the market risk of option positions

Table 3.7 Comparison of VaR methods.

	Historical	Simulation	Analytic
Ease of implemenation			
Easy to aggregate risk across markets	Yes	Yes	Yes
Data available at no charge	No	No	Yes
Ease of programming (spreadsheet)	Easiest	Hardest	Medium
Distributions for market factors			
Must specific distributions be assumed?	No	Yes	Yes
Are actual volatilities and correlations used?	Yes	Possible	Yes
Handling of individual instruments			
Are pricing models required?	Yes	Yes	No
Is it necessary to map instruments?	No	No	Yes
Accurate handling of options	Yes	Yes	No
Communication with senior management			
Ease of explanation	Easiest	Medium	Hardest
Can sensitivity analyses be done?	No	Yes	Some

Source: Smitson/Minton, Risk.

based on delta (or delta and gamma). This results in inaccurate risk estimates for large changes in the price of the underlying; it also ignores the potential effect of changes in the volatility of the underlying. The historic and simulation methods can account for changes in all the market factors that affect an option price, and the revaluation process allows the market risk of options to be more accurately measured for larger changes in market factors.

A comparison of the three methodologies is presented at Table 3.7, summarised from Risk in November 1997.

Choosing between methods

The composition of a bank's portfolio is a prime factor in deciding which method to implement. For portfolios with no options the analytic method may be most suitable because it does not require pricing models. Publicly available software and data (e.g., RiskMetrics) makes installation simpler.

The historical or simulation methods are more appropriate for portfolios with option positions. The historical method is conceptually simple and the required pricing models are often available as add-ins for spreadsheet packages. The main obstacle to using the simulation method is the complex task of doing Monte Carlo simulations; although the software is available the process is time-consuming.

RiskMetrics

RiskMetrics was launched by JP Morgan in 1994. Its approach is to assume that changes in prices and yields of financial instruments follow the normal distribution. Given this assumption volatility can be expressed in terms of the standard deviation from the mean. RiskMetrics uses 1.645 (usually rounded to 1.65) standard deviations as its measure of risk, which encompasses 95% of occurrences (in a one-tailed test, or the 'negative' or loss end of the curve).

The assumptions behind RiskMetrics give rise to these two consequences:

- by setting a confidence level of 95%, we say that we are prepared to accept a 5% chance that the market will move beyond our parameters; on 1 day in 20 the market will move more than we predict;
- we accept the risk that in reality some market prices, such as FX rates, move in a non-normal manner; there is considerable evidence that many rates display 'fat tails', implying that the number and size of large movements is higher than forecast by a normal distribution.

The analytical approach of RiskMetrics is a direct application of modern portfolio theory and is summarised by the following equation, which we encountered earlier:

$$\sigma_p^2 = \sum_{i=1}^{n} (\alpha_i \cdot \sigma_i)^2 + 2 \sum_{i=1}^{n} \sum_{i=1}^{n} \alpha_i \alpha_j \rho_{ij} \sigma_i \sigma_j$$

where
- σ_p^2 = Variance for the entire portfolio;
- α_i = Portfolio weighting for asset i;
- σ_i^2 = Variance of the logarithmic return of asset i;
- ρ_{ij} = Correlation between the logarithmic return of asset i and of asset j;
- n = Number of assets in the portfolio.

This equation essentially states that total portfolio risk is a function of two types of factors:

- the volatility of each distinct asset in the portfolio, denoted by σ_i and σ_j; and
- the correlations between assets, denoted by ρ_{ij}.

Box 3.1   Technical addendum.

The calculation of portfolio standard deviations using an equally weighted moving average approach is given by:

$$\sigma_t = \sqrt{\frac{1}{(k-1)} \sum_{s=t-k}^{t-1} (x_s - \mu)^2}$$

where

σ_t = Estimated standard deviation of the portfolio at beginning of the time period t;

k = Number of days in the observation period;

x_s = Change in portfolio value on day s;

μ = Mean change in the portfolio value.

The formula for the portfolio standard deviation under an exponentially weighted moving average approach is represented by:

$$\sigma_t = \sqrt{(1-\lambda) \sum_{s=t-k}^{t-1} (x_s - \mu)^2}$$

The parameter λ, referred to as the 'decay factor', determines the rate at which the weights on past observations decay as they become more distant.

Exponentially weighted moving averages emphasise recent observations by using weighted averages of squared deviations. They aim to capture short-term movements in volatility.

Given the assumption of normality of returns we can estimate within a certain level of confidence the range over which the portfolio will fluctuate on a daily, weekly, monthly and annual basis.

For example, for a portfolio with no more than a 5% chance that its market value will decrease by more than £1 million over a 1-day period, the VaR is £1 million.

RiskMetrics defines market risk, first, in terms of absolute market risk: the estimate of total loss expressed in currency terms (i.e., dollars or pounds of risk). Second, it defines risk in terms of a time horizon. Its daily earnings at risk $(DEaR)$ number is defined as the expected loss over a 1-day horizon. VaR itself measures the potential loss over a longer horizon, such as 1 month.

RiskMetrics bases its estimates of volatility and correlations on historical data. As we saw in the previous section, this is a methodological choice. There are alternative approaches to estimating future volatility: subjective forecasts can be used, alternatively implied volatilities from exchange-traded instruments can be used. Of course, many instruments are not exchange-traded, nor is the forecasting power of implied volatility necessarily greater than historical volatility. RiskMetrics uses exponentially weighted moving averages of historical rate movements. Generally, 75 days' worth of data are used, and the weighting means that newer data are given more emphasis than older data. This ensures that the volatility estimates respond quickly to market shocks, but also that they gradually revert back to more normal levels. However, in the immediate aftermath of a significant correction, the volatility figure may be unrealistically high.

To calculate a single position VaR example in simple fashion, consider Example 3.2.

Example 3.2   VaR calculation.

VaR	Amount of position $*$ Volatility of instrument;
Volatility	% of value which may be lost with a certain possibility (e.g., 95%);
Position	A bond trader is long of $40 million US 10-year Treasury benchmark;
Market risk	US 10-year volatility is 0.932%;
VaR =	$40 million $* 0.932\% = \$372,800$.

For a two-position VaR example the portfolio now needs to consider correlations and the following expression is applied:

$$VaR = \sqrt{VaR_1^2 + VaR_2^2 + 2\rho VaR_1 VaR_2}$$

where VaR_1 = Value-at-risk for Instrument 1;
        VaR_2 = Value-at-risk for Instrument 2;
        ρ = Correlation between the price movements of Instrument 1 and 2.

The individual VaRs are calculated as before.

Essentially, RiskMetrics follows the procedure detailed in the previous section for analytic method VaR estimates.

The core of RiskMetrics is:

- a method mapping position, forecasting volatilities and correlations, and risk estimation;
- a daily updated set of estimated volatilities and correlations of rates and prices.

The DEaR and VaR are the maximum estimated loss in market value of a given position that can be expected to be incurred with 95% certainty until the position can be neutralised or reassessed.

Assessment

The key technical assumptions made by RiskMetrics are:

- conditional multivariate normality of returns and assets;
- exponentially weighted moving average forecasts of volatility (as against GARCH or stochastic models);
- variance–covariance method of calculation (as against historical simulation).

The key limitations are:

- limited applicability to options and non-linear positions generally;
- simplicity of its mapping process, assuming cash flows on standardised grid points on the time line;
- like any VaR model, no coverage of liquidity risk, funding risk, credit risk or operational risk.

Comparison with the historical approach

The historical approach is preferred in some firms because of its simplicity. It differs from RiskMetrics in three respects:

- it makes no explicit assumption about the variances of portfolio assets and the correlations between them;
- it makes no assumptions about the shape of the distribution of asset returns, including no assumption of normality;
- it requires no simplification or mapping of cash flows.

To calculate VaR using this approach all that is required is a historical record of the daily profit and loss (*p&l*) of the portfolio under
consideration. Hence, a major strength of the historical approach is
the minimal analytical capability required. An additional benefit is
the lack of cash flow mapping. The simplification process can create
substantial risk distortion, particularly if there are options in the
portfolio. Under RiskMetrics, options are converted into their delta
equivalents.

The main drawback of the historical approach is that since it is based
strictly on the past it is not useful for scenario analysis. With Risk-
Metrics we can alter the assumed variances and correlations to see
how the VaR would be affected. This is not possible under the historical approach.

Other market methodologies

Following the introduction of RiskMetrics other banks introduced
their own VaR models into the market.

Charisma

The Charisma model was developed by Chase Manhattan in 1996.
Charisma (*Chase Risk Management Analyser*) constructs distributions of probable future price changes using historical data. The
model identifies portfolio exposure to specific risks such as FX
and interest rate volatility, and identifies the price changes in
those markets for each of the last 100 days. The portfolio is then
revalued as if each price change occurred from today's price level,
thus creating 100 possible changes to the portfolio's value. From
these numbers the bank's risk manager can determine a VaR number
corresponding to a given confidence level. The model uses a 97.5%
confidence level, meaning that losses are not expected to exceed the
VaR number in more than 2.5% of cases or once in every 40 days.

The model's simplicity is viewed by some as advantageous when
descriptions of it are given to board-level management. Compare the
Charisma model with RiskMetrics and its variance–covariance approach. RiskMetrics VaR number uses historic volatility and correlation data to predict how the market will move in the future. As we
have noted RiskMetrics exponentially weights historical returns
such that newer data are given more emphasis than older data.

(Note that Bloomberg's VaR calculator, while based on RiskMetrics, allows users the option of setting their own weighting adjustment, should they choose to.) Charisma, because it uses *actual* price changes rather than average volatilities, does not adjust data. Of course, the main difference between the two models is that the variance–covariance approach must assume that portfolio returns follow a normal distribution. In fact, returns in practice often exhibit skewed return, or 'fat tails' in the picture of the distribution, referred to as *leptokurtosis*. Because instruments such as options exhibit a greater degree of skewed returns than others, banks often calculate two VaR numbers, one for the options portfolio and one for the remainder of the book.

PrimeRisk

PrimeRisk was introduced by Credit Suisse First Boston (*CSFB*) in 1996. The model is a forecasting model for volatilities and correlations. It produces risk parameters such as volatilities, prices and zero-coupon yield curves, while a front-end interface known as PrimeClear calculates the VaR. PrimeRisk uses different volatility models for different markets. Individually tailored volatility models for each market are used to help improve forecasting accuracy. This differs from RiskMetrics which uses an identical volatility model for all markets.

The model also weights data; PrimeRisk uses fractional exponential weighting of its historical data, giving lower weightings to recent and distant days and increased weight to intermediate days' data. According to CSFB (which back-tested the model against actual market results) this method results in up to a 10% lower level of forecasting error than the simple exponential method as used by RiskMetrics.

USE OF VaR MODELS

The different VaR methodologies available provide a range of estimates for any one portfolio. Here we summarise the variances that resulted from a study conducted by T. S. Beder in *Financial Analysts Journal*, September/October 1995.

Table 3.8 VaR model approaches.

No.	Simulation type	Database/Correlation method	Holding period
1	Historical	Previous 100 days	1 day
2	Historical	Previous 250 days	1 day
3	Monte Carlo	Historical, RiskMetrics correlations	1 day
4	Historical	Previous 100 days	2 weeks
5	Historical	Previous 250 days	2 weeks
6	Monte Carlo	Historical, RiskMetrics correlations	2 weeks

Hypothetical portfolio VaR testing

The results of applying two methodologies to three hypothetical portfolios is given below. For the same portfolio the calculated VaR ranged from 100 to 1400.

The types of calculation performed are stated in Table 3.8.

The three portfolios were:

(1) a long position in 2-year and 10-year US Treasury strips;
(2) a long position in the S&P 500 equity index contract plus long and short options on the same contract;
(3) a combination of the first two portfolios.

The results of the VaR calculation are shown in Table 3.9.

VaR as percentage of portfolio

For Portfolio 1, the plain vanilla portfolio, the VaR ranged from 0.20% of the portfolio to 2.61%; the highest measure of risk is thus 13 times the lowest. For Portfolio 2 the VaR ranged from 0.69% to 3.95%, a variation of over five times, while for Portfolio 3 the range was from 0.48% to 3.00%, a six-fold variation.

Bank of England comparison of VaR models

The Bank of England (*BoE*) carried out an analysis of different types of VaR models, in order to ascertain if certain methodologies were more consistently accurate than others (see the Bank's *Working Paper*

Table 3.9 Comparison of VaR models.

	95% confidence	99% confidence
Portfolio 1		
1	0.49	0.67
2	0.83	1.29
3	0.63	0.88
4	0.20	0.82
5	1.70	2.14
6	1.82	2.61
Portfolio 2		
1	0.69	1.26
2	0.91	1.30
3	0.85	1.07
4	2.31	3.48
5	3.89	3.94
6	3.92	3.95
Portfolio 3		
1	0.48	0.73
2	0.74	1.08
3	0.57	0.77
4	1.24	1.71
5	2.56	2.89
6	2.51	3.00

No. 79). It classified the models tested as two types:

- *Parametric* VaR models, in which the distribution of asset returns is estimated from historic data. Such models, as we have already stated, assume that returns are stationary, normally distributed and independent over time.
- *Simulation* models, which calculate the losses that would have been experienced on a particular portfolio in previous 24-hour periods (using a run of historical returns data) and the loss that is exceeded on a given percentage of days in the sample. These non-parametric models make no assumptions about distribution of returns, other than their independence over time.

In testing the models, the BoE selected a range of parameters to test, concerning (a) the timescale of the historic data selected (T), (b) the weighting scheme adopted for historic data – weighting the data using ($\lambda_0, \lambda_1, \ldots, \lambda_{T-1}$) – and (c) whether the mean should be estimated using the sample mean, $\sum_{j=0}^{T-1} r_{t-T+j}/T$, or set to 0 as has been suggested in other empirical work.

Results of BoE testing

The BoE compared the results produced by parametric and non-parametric VaR models. As non-parametric models do not produce a time series of volatility forecast errors, testing was restricted to a comparison of the 'tail probabilities' that the two types of models produce; that is, the frequency of the tail in the distribution of returns (losses) exceeding the 1% cut-off level more than 1% of the time. As, in theory, the models tested are calculating VaR estimates based on a 99% confidence interval, tail sizes exceeding 1% indicate the inaccuracy of the model. This is to be expected, given the widely documented occurrence of leptokurtosis of interest rates and stock returns; that is, the incidence of 'fat-tailed' distributions.

Table 3.10, reproduced from the BoE *Quarterly Bulletin* of August 1998, shows the results for data window lengths ranging from 6 months to 24 months. We show the results for three portfolios, the first two a combination of FX and bond positions, and the third portfolio with the same instruments in addition to a basket of equities.

The results in Table 3.10 suggest that calculating the 1-day and 10-day VaR cut-off points from short data windows is inadvisable because small-sample biases are substantial. For longer data windows the non-parametric approach for 1-day returns consistently outperforms the parametric model, as the tail probabilities are matched more accurately. With the parametric approach the tail probabilities calculated using different lag lengths consistently exceed the 1% level. This reflects the skewed, rather than orthodox normal, distribution of financial returns. For the 10-day returns the non-parametric approach appears to perform worse than the parametric VaR estimates for portfolios in certain cases.

SUMMARY

The different VaR calculations all produce different estimates for VaR from the same data. We illustrated how matrices are used to calculate VaR in the variance–covariance approach, which is the one used by RiskMetrics. The benefits of using matrices are that the user

Table 3.10 Parametric and simulation VaR tail probabilities.

	6 months' data	12 months' data	24 months' data
Portfolio 1			
1-day return parametric	1.91	1.58	1.51
10-day return parametric*	0.72	0.99	0.92
1-day return simulation	0.99	1.18	1.18
10-day return simulation**	1.32	1.45	1.65
Portfolio 2			
1-day return parametric	1.32	1.45	1.25
10-day return parametric*	1.12	1.05	1.05
1-day return simulation	0.86	1.18	0.86
10-day return simulation**	1.32	1.58	1.18
Portfolio 3			
1-day return parametric	1.65	1.71	1.38
10-day return parametric*	1.12	1.18	0.92
1-day return simulation	0.72	1.38	0.92
10-day return simulation**	1.58	1.38	1.25

*Calculated by multiplying the 1-day VaR estimate by the square root of 10.
**Calculated by estimating the VaR from the portfolio losses over 10-day periods.

Source: BoE, 1998.

can set up a weighting matrix, containing all the assets in the trading book, a correlation matrix, which contains the correlations of one asset with all the other assets in the portfolio, and a volatility matrix. The user then multiplies the matrices to calculate the standard deviation of the portfolio, which is then used to obtain the portfolio VaR.

The variance–covariance approach is based on the use of matrices to calculate VaR. In theory, using this approach the benefits of diversification are captured because the VaR of the portfolio as a whole tend to be lower than the sum of all the individual VaR numbers. In our illustration we saw that the order in which matrices are multiplied is important, as is their composition. For instance, in the volatility matrix the standard deviations are placed in the diagonal, while the other cells contain 0 values. Thus, in a ten-asset portfolio, we would set a 10 × 10 matrix and enter the volatility values along the diagonals. The remaining cells in the matrix would contain 0s. The correlation matrix contains '1' values along the diagonals (because the correlation of an asset with itself is 1), and the correlation coefficients in the other cells. Once we have calculated the variance–covariance matrix, we use the weighting matrix to calculate the portfolio standard deviation. The weighting matrix is always one row, while the number of columns will be the number of assets in the portfolio.

Possibly the easiest VaR method to use is the variance–covariance one. It is straightforward to implement because the datasets required in its calculation, for liquid currencies, are already available from the RiskMetrics website (www.riskmetrics.com). This holds volatility and correlation data for all major currencies and assets. A bank setting up a VaR system for the first time need only construct a weighting matrix for its assets, and then use the volatility and correlations available from the Internet. The drawbacks of the approach are that it assumes constant volatilities, and that asset returns follow a normal distribution. It has been observed that the occurrence of market crashes occurs more frequently than is implied by a normal distribution, causing the measurement to be biased. However, the approach is popular with practitioners because it is easy to implement and explain.

The historical approach is also easy to understand. In this method, risk managers keep a historical record of the daily p&l of the portfolio and then calculate the fifth percentile cut-off for a 95% VaR figure. The historical approach uses actual market data, unlike, say, Risk-Metrics whose volatilities and correlations are estimates based on averages over a specified period of time. In extreme situations, such as market corrections or crashes, average values do not hold and so the variance–covariance approach will produce an unrealistic result. The historical method uses actual results to make its calculation, so recent past market events are picked up more accurately. The historical method also does not require any mapping of cash flows to grid points. The mapping approach is straightforward for plain vanilla instruments but makes certain assumptions that are not realistic for more exotic instruments such as options. The weakness of the historical approach is that it does not account for changes in portfolio weightings over time. However, this shortcoming can be overcome using a more complex method known as *historical simulation*. This approach not only uses the current composition of the portfolio, but also historical market data. As it is a simulation it requires a large amount of computer resources. Put simply, if a current portfolio was composed of 80% of Asset A and 20% of

Asset B, the user would obtain the asset prices of A and B over a specified period in the past – say, the last 1000 days – and for each day calculate the value of the portfolio, using the 80 : 20 weightings and keeping them constant. The VaR measure is then calculated as before.

Chapter

4

....

VALUE-AT-RISK FOR FIXED INTEREST INSTRUMENTS

This chapter discusses market risk for fixed income products. The measures described in the first section are regarded as being for 'first-order risk'. Since the advent of value-at-risk (*VaR*), risk managers and traders have been using both types of measure to quantify market exposure. In this chapter we consider calculation of VaR for a fixed interest product. We also note that credit derivatives are now a significant segment of the fixed income markets.

FIXED INCOME PRODUCTS

We consider the basic building blocks of a bond, which we break down as a series of cash flows. Before that, we discuss essential background on bond pricing and duration.

Bond valuation

A vanilla bond pays a fixed rate of interest (coupon) annually or semi-annually, or very rarely quarterly. The *fair price* of such a bond is given by the discounted present value of the total cash flow stream, using a market-determined discount rate.

Yield to maturity (*YTM*) is the most frequently used measure of return from holding a bond. The YTM is equivalent to the *internal rate of return* on the bond, the rate that equates the value of the discounted cash flows on the bond to its current price. The YTM equation for a bond paying semi-annual coupons is:

$$P = \sum_{t=1}^{2T} \frac{C/2}{\left(1+\frac{1}{2}r\right)^t} + \frac{M}{\left(1+\frac{1}{2}r\right)^{2T}} \qquad (4.1)$$

where P = Fair price of bond;
          C = Coupon;
          M = Redemption payment (par);
          T = Number of years to maturity;
          r = Required rate of return on the bond.

The solution to this equation cannot be found analytically and has to be solved through iteration; that is, by estimating the yield from two trial values for r, then solving by using the formula for linear interpolation.

In practice, one can use the Excel function references '=PRICE' and '=YIELD' to work out a bond price or yield given one or the other.

Table 4.1 Spreadsheet calculation of bond price or yield using an Excel function reference.

B	C	D	E
3	**5% 2016 corporate bond**		
4			
5			
6	06/01/2006 settlement date		
7	15/02/2016 maturity date		
8	5% coupon		
9	98.95 price		
10	100 par		
11	2 semi annual coupon		
12	4 30/360 day-count		
13			
14			
15	YIELD 5.134%		0.05132928
16			
17	PRICE 98.95642289		
18			
19	DURATION 7.888769069		
20			

YIELD   =YIELD(C6,C7,C8,C9,C10,C11,C12)

PRICE   =PRICE(C6,C7,C8,E15,C10,C11,C12)

DURATION =DURATION(C6,C7,C8,D15,C11,C12)

This is demonstrated in Table 4.1 for a plain vanilla semi-annual bullet bond.

While YTM is the most commonly used measure of yield, it has one major disadvantage. The effect of this means that in practice the measure itself will not equal the actual return from holding the bond, even if it is held to maturity. The disadvantage is that implicit in the calculation of the YTM is the assumption that each coupon payment as it becomes due is reinvested at the rate r. This is clearly unlikely, due to the fluctuations in interest rates over time and as the bond approaches maturity.

The bond price equation has illustrated the relationship between a bond's price and discount rate (the yield measure). The percentage increase in price when yields decline is greater than the percentage decrease when yields rise. This is due to the convex relationship, when plotted on a graph, between price and yield.

The sensitivity of a bond to changes in interest rate is measured by *duration* and *modified duration*. Duration is the weighted average maturity of a bond, using the discounted cash flows of the bond as weights.

Duration

The measure of interest rate risk typically used by bond analysts is called 'duration'. Duration is defined as:

The weighted average time until the receipt of cash flows from an instrument, where the weights are the present values of cash flows.

It was developed by Macaulay in 1938, and is sometimes referred to as 'Macaulay's duration'.

Formally, we can write duration as the following expression:

$$D = \frac{\sum_{t=1}^{n} \frac{tC_t}{(1+r)^t}}{P} \tag{4.2}$$

where $D = $ Duration;
$P = $ Price of the bond;
$C_t = $ Cash flow at time t;
$r = $ Yield to maturity.

In the case of a zero-coupon bond there is only one cash flow, the payment at maturity. Therefore, for zero-coupon bonds the duration is always equal to the maturity of the bond.

Example 4.1   Duration calculation.

Consider a Eurobond with 8% coupon, maturing in 5 years' time and priced (present-valued) at 100, thus giving a YTM of 8%.

Present value is calculated using the standard formula:

$$\frac{C}{(1+r)n}$$

Cash flow	PV at 8% yield	Time (t)	$PV \times t$
8	7.41	1	7.41
8	6.86	2	3.72
8	6.35	3	19.05
8	5.88	4	23.52
108	73.50	5	367.51
	100.00		**431.21**

Duration is $\dfrac{431.21}{100}$ which equals 4.31 years

This also illustrates that for a coupon-bearing bond the duration is always less than for the corresponding maturity zero-coupon bond. The 5-year coupon bond in our example has a duration of 4.31 years; the zero-coupon bond would have a duration of 5 years. Duration also varies with coupon, yield and maturity. Figure 4.1 illustrates the price sensitivity profile for a straight bond.

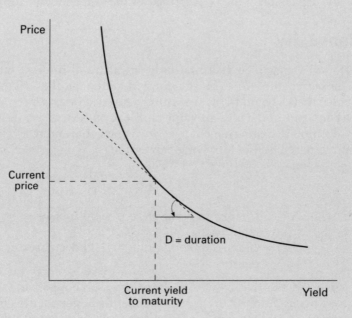

Figure 4.1 Bond price/yield profile.

Modified duration

Duration is important as it measures the interest rate elasticity of the bond price and is therefore a measure of interest rate risk. The lower the duration the less responsive is the bond's value to interest rate moves. *Modified duration* measures the sensitivity of the bond's price to changes in the yield curve. It is related to duration as follows:

$$MD = \frac{D}{1+r} \qquad (4.3)$$

where MD = Modified duration;
          r = Yield to maturity.

In our example where D is 4.31 years and the yield is 8%, then:

$$MD = \frac{4.31}{1.08} = 3.99$$

Modified duration measures the proportionate impact on the price of the bond of a change in yield. In our example the modified duration is 3.99; if yield rises by 1% the bond price falls by 3.99%.

The duration and modified duration formulae are obtained via a Taylor expansion. This is described in the Appendix (p. 155).

Convexity

Duration is regarded as a first-order measure of interest rate risk: it measures the *slope* of the present value profile (Figure 4.1). *Convexity* is a second-order measure of interest rate risk: it measures the curvature of the present value profile. Convexity describes how a bond's modified duration changes with respect to interest rates. It is approximated by the following expression:

$$\text{Convexity} = 10^8 \left(\frac{\Delta P'_d}{\Delta P_d} + \frac{\Delta P''_d}{P_d} \right) \qquad (4.4)$$

where $\Delta P'_d$ = Change in bond price if yield increases by 1 basis point (0.01);
          $\Delta P''_d$ = Change in bond price if yield decreases by 1 basis point.

It can be shown that convexity decreases with coupon and yield. It becomes a useful measure when considering larger changes in yield. Duration, as a linear approximation to a curved present value profile, is a reasonable estimate for small changes in yield. For large moves this linear approximation will be inaccurate if convexity is high. A bond with higher convexity will outperform one of lower convexity whatever happens to interest rates. The price of such a bond will fall by less for a given rise in yield, and will rise by more if yields fall, than that of a bond of lower convexity.

INTEREST RATE PRODUCTS

For newcomers we introduce a simple forward rate instrument as a prelude to discussing a simple bond portfolio.

Forward rate agreements

A forward rate agreement (FRA) is a simple derivative contract that essentially allows banks or corporates to hedge against future interest rate exposure. Say that a corporate expects to borrow funds in 6 months' time, but at the rate prevailing at that time. To assist its budgeting process, it can fix the rate today (or, if it expects interest rates to worsen in 6 months' time, it can deal today) by buying an FRA. If rates indeed have risen in 6 months' time, the extra interest the corporate will pay on the loan will be compensated by the money it receives on the FRA.[1] No money changes hands at the start of an FRA transaction, only the difference in interest between the transacted rate and the rate at 'fixing' (maturity) is paid or received.

We illustrate FRAs with an example. Assume a corporate expects to receive £10 million in 3 months' time as working capital. These funds are not expected to be needed until 3 months after receipt, so they will be placed on deposit until then. The company can simply wait until then and deal, but let us suppose it expects interest rates to have dropped by then, and so wishes to lock in a deposit rate now. The bank it deals with will write a ticket for a forward deposit, and the rate it quotes will be the 3-month rate in 3 months' time; that is, the 3-month forward–forward rate. In FRA terms this would be known as a 'threes–sixes' or '3v6' FRA.

If the 3-month rate is 5.25% and 6-month rate is 5.75%, the forward rate is the 'breakeven' rate for 3-month money in 3 months' time.

---

[1] 'Buying' a FRA is, in effect, 'borrowing' money, so if I buy a FRA at 6% and the rate on settlement is 7% I will have made the 1% difference because, in effect, I have fixed my borrowing at the lower rate.

Table 4.2 FRA rate calculation.

A1	B	C	D	E	F	G	H
2	3-month rate	5.25%					
3	6-month rate	5.75%					
4							
5			Days		Cashflow	Borrow for 3 months	Depo for 6 months
6	Today	09-Jan-06			£10,000,000.00	£9,870,800.68	-£9,870,800.68
7		10-Apr-06	91			£10,000,000.00	
8		10-Jul-06	182		-£10,153,808.71		£10,153,808.71
9							
10							
11				Implied return		1.5381%	
12				Days		91	
13				Forward-forward rate		6.1693%	
14							
15							

3-month   5.25%   6.169% fwd-fwd rate

6-month   5.75%

Table 4.3 Excel spreadsheet formulae for Table 4.1.

A1	B	C	D	E	F	G	H
2	3-month rate	5.25%					
3	6-month rate	5.75%					
4							
5			Days		Cashflow	Borrow for 3 months	Depo for 6 months
6	Today 09-Jan-06						=-G6
7		=C6+91	91		£10,000,000.00	=F7/(1+D7/365*C2)	
8		=C6+182	182		=-H8	=G6*(1+C2*D7/365)	=-H6*(1+D8/365*C3)
9							
10							
11					Implied return	=F8/-F7-1	
12					Days	=D8-D7	
13					Forward-forward rate	=365/G12*G11	
14							
15							

The calculation for this is shown in Table 4.2. Think of the calculation in terms of what the bank would do to hedge this exposure: it would borrow £9,870,800.68, which is the present value of £10 million in 3 months' time, and place this on deposit for 6 months. The FRA rate (assuming no bid–offer spreads) is 6.17% and is shown in cell G13 in Table 4.2. The Excel formulae are shown in Table 4.3 (previous page).

Fixed income portfolio

A bond is a series of cash flows (the coupons) and a final coupon and redemption payment. We can view the package as a series of FRAs, in effect. We illustrate bonds by looking at an hypothetical simple bond portfolio comprised of three bonds. This is shown at Table 4.4. Assume the date is 9 January 2006 and the bonds have precise terms to maturity.

Table 4.5 (see p. 71) shows the bond cash flows, their present values based on an assumed zero-coupon term structure and the total market value of the portfolio. Table 4.6 shows the undiversified VaR for this portfolio, which is simply the total of the present values multiplied by their volatility.

Table 4.4 Hypothetical Eurobond portfolio.

	5% Eurobond 2008	6% Eurobond 2007	4.25% Eurobond 2010
Holding	$10 million	$5 million	$5 million

Table 4.6 Undiversified VaR for portfolio.

Cash flow date	Cash flows	Present values	Volatilities	Undiversified VaR
1	6,012,500.00	5,726,190.48	0.315%	18,037.50
2	10,712,500.00	9,670,448.71	0.335%	32,396.00
3	212,500.00	180,967.90	0.374%	676.82
4	212,500.00	169,276.04	0.407%	688.95
5	5,212,500.00	3,895,083.23	0.528%	20,566.04
			Totals	72,365.31

Table 4.5 Bond portfolio valuation.

Term structure
1y	5.00%
2y	5.25%
3y	5.50%
4y	5.85%
5y	6.00%

	Cash flows			Discount factors	Present values			Totals
Cash flow date	5% 2008	6% 2007	4.25% 2010		6% 2007	5% 2008	4.25% 2010	
1	500,000.00	5,300,000.00	212,500.00	0.9523810	5,047,619.05	476,190.48	202,380.95	5,726,190.48
2	10,500,000.00		212,500.00	0.9027257	0.00	9,478,619.51	191,829.20	9,670,448.71
3			212,500.00	0.8516137			180,967.90	180,967.90
4			212,500.00	0.7965931			169,276.04	169,276.04
5			5,212,500.00	0.7472582			3,895,083.23	3,895,083.23
Totals					5,047,619.05	9,954,809.98	4,639,537.32	
Portfolio total								19,641,966.35

Table 4.7   Undiversified VaR for 3v6 FRA.

Cash flow	Term (days)	Cash rate	Interest rate volatilities	Present value	Undiversified VaR
10,000,000	91	5.38%	0.14%	9,867,765	13,815
10,144,536	182	5.63%	0.21%	9,867,765	20,722

To calculate the diversified VaR we apply the matrix technique described in the previous chapter, using the bond correlations to obtain a portfolio variance and then the portfolio VaR.

APPLYING VaR FOR A FRA

The VaR calculation for a FRA follows the same principles reviewed in Chapter 3. As we saw earlier the derivation of a FRA rate is based on the principle of what it would cost for a bank that traded one to hedge it; this is known as the 'breakeven' rate. So a bank that has bought 3v6 FRA (remember, this is called a 'threes–sixes FRA') has effectively borrowed funds for 3 months and placed the funds on deposit for 6 months. Therefore, a FRA is best viewed as a combination of an asset and a liability, and that is how it is valued. So, a long position in a 3v6 FRA is valued as the present value of a 3-month cash flow asset and the present value of a 6-month cash flow liability, using the 3-month and 6-month deposit rates. The net present value is taken, of course, because one cash flow is an asset and the other a liability.

Consider a 3v6 FRA that has been dealt at 5.797%, the 3-month forward–forward rate. The value of its constituent (notional) cash flows is shown in Table 4.7. The 3-month and 6-month rates are cash rates in the market, while the interest rate volatilities have been obtained from the RiskMetrics website.[2] The details are summarised in Table 4.7.

The undiversified VaR is the sum of the individual VaR values, and is £34,537. It has little value in the case of a FRA, however, and would overstate the true VaR, because a FRA is made up of a notional asset and liability, so a fall in the value of one would see a rise in the value

---

[2]RiskMetrics was hived off JPMorgan in 1997 and is now a separate, independent legal entity.

VaR weighting transposed   Correlation matrix

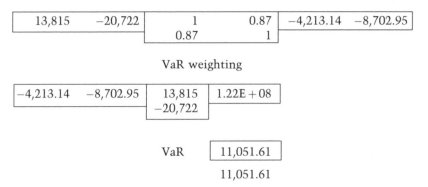

Figure 4.2 Diversified VaR calculation for 3v6 FRA, correlation coefficient 0.87.

of the other. Unless a practitioner was expecting 3-month rates to go in an opposite direction to 6-month rates, there is an element of diversification benefit. There is a high correlation between the two rates, so the more logical approach is to calculate a diversified VaR measure.

For an instrument such as a FRA, the fact that the two rates used in calculating the FRA rate are closely positively correlated will mean that the diversification effect will be to reduce the VaR estimate, because the FRA is composed notionally of an asset and a liability. From the values in Table 4.7, therefore, the 6-month VaR is actually a negative value (if the bank had sold the FRA, the 3-month VaR would have the negative value). To calculate the diversified VaR then requires the correlation between the two interest rates, which may be obtained from the RiskMetrics dataset. This is observed to be 0.87. This value is entered into a 2 × 2 correlation matrix and used to calculate the diversified VaR in the normal way. The procedure is:

- transpose the weighting VaR matrix to turn it into a 2 × 1 matrix;
- multiply this by the correlation matrix;
- multiply the result by the original 1 × 2 weighting matrix;
- this gives us the variance; the VaR is the square root of this value.

The result is an diversified VaR of £11,051. The matrix procedure is shown at Figure 4.2.

VaR FOR AN INTEREST RATE SWAP

An interest rate swap is essentially a series of FRAs. To calculate a variance–covariance VaR for an interest rate swap, we use the process described earlier for a FRA. There are more cash flows that go to make up the undiversified VaR, as the swap is a strip of FRAs. In a plain vanilla interest rate swap, one party pays fixed rate interest on an annual or semi-annual basis, and receives floating rate interest, while the other party pays floating rate interest payments and receives fixed rate interest. Interest payments are calculated on a notional sum, which does not change hands, and only interest payments are exchanged. In practice, it is the net difference between the two payments that is transferred.

The fixed rate on an interest rate swap is the breakeven rate that equates the present value of the fixed rate payments to the present value of the floating rate payments; as the floating rate payments are linked to a reference rate such as the London Interbank Offered Rate (*LIBOR*), we do not know what they will be, but we use the forward rate applicable to each future floating payment date to calculate what it would be if we were to fix it today. The forward rate is calculated from zero-coupon rates today. A 'long' position in a swap is to pay fixed and receive floating, and is conceptually the same as being short in a fixed-coupon bond and being long in a floating-rate bond; in effect, the long is 'borrowing' money, so a rise in the fixed rate will result in a rise in the value of the swap. A 'short' position is receiving fixed and paying floating, so a rise in interest rates results in a fall in the value of the swap. This is conceptually similar to a long position in a fixed rate bond and a short position in a floating rate bond.

Describing an interest rate swap in conceptual terms of fixed and floating rate bonds gives some idea as to how it is treated for VaR purposes. The coupon on a floating rate bond is reset periodically in line with the stated reference rate, usually LIBOR. Therefore, the duration of a floating rate bond is very low, and conceptually the bond may be viewed as being the equivalent of a bank deposit, which receives interest payable at a variable rate. For market risk purposes,[3] the risk exposure of a bank deposit is nil, because its present value is not affected by changes in market interest rates. Similarly, the risk

---

[3] We emphasise for *market* risk purposes; the credit risk exposure for a floating rate bond position is a function of the credit quality of the issuer.

Table 4.8   Fixed rate leg of 5-year interest rate swap and undiversified VaR.

Pay date	Swap rate	Principal	Coupon	Coupon present value	Volatility	Undiversified VaR
	(%)	(£)	(£)	(£)	(%)	
07-Jun-00	6.73	10,000,000	337,421	327,564	0.05	164
07-Dec-00	6.73	10,000,000	337,421	315,452	0.05	158
07-Jun-01	6.73	10,000,000	335,578	303,251	0.10	303
07-Dec-01	6.73	10,000,000	337,421	294,898	0.11	324
07-Jun-02	6.73	10,000,000	335,578	283,143	0.20	566
09-Dec-02	6.73	10,000,000	341,109	277,783	0.35	972
09-Jun-03	6.73	10,000,000	335,578	264,360	0.33	872
08-Dec-03	6.73	10,000,000	335,578	256,043	0.45	1,152
07-Jun-04	6.73	10,000,000	335,578	248,155	0.57	1,414
07-Dec-04	6.73	10,000,000	337,421	242,161	1.90	4,601
					Total	**10,526**

exposure of a floating rate bond is very low and to all intents and purposes its VaR may be regarded as 0. This leaves only the fixed rate leg of a swap to measure for VaR purposes.

Table 4.8 shows the fixed rate leg of a 5-year interest rate swap of the following terms:

Trade date	3 December 1999
Effective date	7 December 1999
Maturity	7 December 2004
Nominal	GBP10 million
Fixed rate	6.73%
Day-count	Act/365
Semi-annual	

To calculate the undiversified VaR we use the volatility rate for each term interest rate; this may be obtained from RiskMetrics website, for instance. Note that the RiskMetrics dataset supports only liquid currencies; for example, data on volatility and correlation is not available for certain emerging market economies. Below we show the VaR for each payment; the sum of all the payments constitutes the undiversified VaR. We then require the correlation matrix for the interest rates, and this is used to calculate the diversified VaR. The weighting matrix contains the individual term VaR values, which must be transposed before being multiplied by the correlation matrix.

Using the volatilities and correlations supplied by RiskMetrics the diversified VaR is shown to be £10,325. This is very close to the undiversified VaR of £10,526. This is not unexpected because the different interest rates are very closely correlated. The matrices are shown at Figure 4.3 (see opposite).

Using VaR to measure market risk exposure for interest rate products enables a risk manager to capture non-parallel shifts in the yield curve, which is an advantage over the traditional duration measure and interest rate gap measure. Therefore, estimating a book's VaR measure is useful not only for the trader and risk manager, but also for senior management, who by using VaR will have a more accurate idea of the risk market exposure of the bank. VaR methodology captures pivotal shifts in the yield curve by using the correlations between different maturity interest rates; this reflects the fact that short-term interest rates and long-term interest rates are not per-fectly positively correlated.

The weighting matrix W is composed of the individual VaR values for each interest rate period in the swap. This is shown in Figure 4.4.

In order to multiply this by the correlation matrix C it needs to be transposed, and this is shown as Figure 4.3(i), the correlation matrix. These data may be obtained from RiskMetrics direct or downloaded from *http://www.Riskmetrics.com*

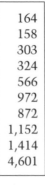

Figure 4.4   Interest rate swap weighting matrix.

(i) **WV transpose**

164	158	303	324	566	972	872	1152	1414	4601

Correlation matrix

1	0.89	0.91	0.92	0.94	0.87	0.91	0.89	0.95	0.97
0.89	1	0.97	0.96	0.95	0.97	0.89	0.91	0.98	0.93
0.91	0.97	1	0.96	0.95	0.94	0.98	0.91	0.92	0.92
0.92	0.96	0.96	1	0.95	0.94	0.95	0.97	0.98	0.97
0.94	0.95	0.95	0.95	1	0.92	0.93	0.93	0.94	0.96
0.87	0.97	0.94	0.94	0.92	1	0.97	0.98	0.95	0.94
0.91	0.89	0.98	0.95	0.93	0.97	1	0.89	0.91	0.95
0.89	0.91	0.91	0.97	0.93	0.98	0.89	1	0.95	0.97
0.95	0.98	0.92	0.98	0.94	0.95	0.91	0.95	1	0.96
0.97	0.93	0.92	0.97	0.96	0.94	0.95	0.97	0.96	1

(ii) **WVC**

9882.823	9880.203	9806.312	10165.1	9990.291	10022.81	9920.518	10094.76	10082.95	10262.1

The usual procedure is then followed, with the WVC matrix multiplied by the weightings matrix; this gives us the variance, from which we calculate the VaR to be £10,325, as shown below:

WCVW	106614498.1
VaR	10325.42968

Figure 4.3 Example of diversified VaR calculation for a 5-year interest rate swap.

APPLYING VaR FOR A BOND FUTURES CONTRACT

As we have seen, there is no consensus on the best way to implement VaR analysis. Most methodologies revolve around estimation of the statistical distribution of asset returns. The main approaches are the variance–covariance methods or *simulation* (or Monte Carlo) methods. Parametric VaR assumes that the distributions of net asset returns are normal. Therefore, the variance–covariance matrix describes the distribution completely. The parametric approach can be summarised by the equation below which we have already encountered; σ_p^2 is the volatility of returns of the portfolio being measured:

$$\sigma_p^2 = \sum (a_i \cdot \sigma_i)^2 + \sum_{i \neq j} \sum_{i \neq j} a_i \cdot a_j \cdot \rho_{ij} \cdot \sigma_i \cdot \sigma_j \qquad (4.5)$$

The equation shows that portfolio risk, as expressed by its variance, is a function of the variance of the return on each instrument in the portfolio as well as on the correlations between each pair of returns. Unless the returns in the portfolio are perfectly correlated (all $\rho_{ij} = 1$) the variance on the portfolio does not equal the simple sum of the variances of the individual positions.

Calculation illustration

We will now illustrate a VaR calculation for the long gilt bond futures contract as traded on LIFFE.

The position in this illustration is a June 1998 long gilt futures contract purchased on 24 May 1998. Assume the closing price that day was 110-00. The contract represents £50,000 nominal of bonds, hence each £1 change in the futures price results in a £500 change in the value of the position (tick value is £15.625, there are 32 ticks per £1).

VaR is estimated in terms of returns (conceptually similar to prices). The return is calculated as:

$$R_t = \frac{P_t - P_t - 1}{P_{t-1}} \cdot 100$$

where R = Daily return;
             P = Price of the instrument.

Table 4.9   Daily price returns.

Date	Futures price	Daily return (%)
24 May 1998 (today)	110-00	
23 May 1998	109-13	0.524702
22 May 1998	110-05	−0.68085
21 May 1998	110-18	0.541928
20 May 1998	109-25	−0.171086
⋮		
31 May 1997	111-08	0.674157
30 May 1997	111-04	0.112486

The daily returns for the bond futures over the last 12 months are shown in Table 4.9.

To calculate the 1-day VaR of this position we need to estimate the mean of the daily returns and the volatility, as measured by the standard deviation. As our portfolio consists of this one position only we do not need to consider correlations.

Assuming the returns follow a normal distribution, 95% of all returns will fall within 1.96 standard deviations of the mean return (using a double-sided, or two-tailed, estimation). If we require a higher confidence level – say, 98% – this will be covered within 2.33 standard deviations of the mean return.

In our example for the long gilt future, we calculate the following:

$$\text{Mean} = -0.00224\%$$

$$\text{Standard deviation} = 0.605074\%$$

This means that for our desired confidence level of 98% all returns would fall between −1.4098% and 1.4098% (rounded to 2 decimal points giving −1.41% and 1.41%) and only 1% of returns will be lower than −1.41% (see Figure 4.5).

The range is obtained by multiplying the standard deviation by 2.33 (i.e., $0.605074 \times 2.33 = 1.4098$), the number of standard deviations required to give us our 98% confidence level.

To convert the negative return of 1.41% to a pounds sterling amount we take the price of the future for the day we are calculating the VaR, which is 110-00.

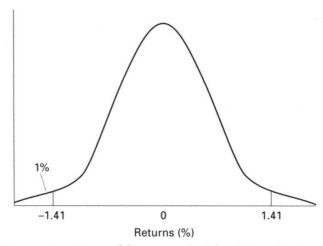

1%

−1.41   0   1.41

Returns (%)

Figure 4.5   1% confidence interval for VaR calculation.

From this we calculate a 1-day VaR at the 98% probability level
(two-tail, representing a price fall) to be:

$$\frac{1.41}{100} \times 110 \times £500 = £775.5$$

If the VaR estimate is accurate the daily loss on this position will
exceed £775.5 on no more than 1 day out of 100.

The risk manager may feel that the 1-day period is too short and that
a 1-week holding period is more appropriate. Assuming that the
returns are serially independent – that is, a return on one day does
not affect the return on any other day – then a property of the
distribution is that the standard deviation increases proportionately
with the square root of time. Therefore, if the 1-day standard
deviation of returns is 0.605 074%, the standard deviation for 1
week (five business days) is:

$$\sqrt{5} \times 0.605\,074 = 1.3530\%$$

This gives us a 1-week VaR at 98% probability level of:

$$\sqrt{5} \times £775.5 = £1,734.07$$

This means that if we held the position for 1 week we should not
expect to lose more than £1,734 more often than 1 week in 100.

The assumptions of normality and serial independence that we
make about the distribution of returns that underlines this analytic

method – of which RiskMetrics is perhaps the best known – allow us to calculate the VaR using any volatility and correlation for any holding period. We in fact do not require the historical returns themselves, which are used in the historical approach.

THE HISTORICAL METHOD

Much empirical research on the statistical properties of asset returns has found deviations from normality. Returns tend to exhibit kurtosis – that is, they are more peaked around the mean and have fatter tails than the normal distribution. Some asset returns tend to be skewed to the left; this indicates a greater incidence of unusually large negative returns, such as crashes, than would be suggested by a normal distribution. For our example we can construct a frequency distribution of the daily returns for the long gilt future between May 1997 and May 1998. The resulting histogram is shown at Figure 4.6, which shows the returns approximating a normal distribution.

A normal curve has been superimposed on the histogram for comparison. The returns do indeed exhibit the typical pattern found in many asset returns, fat tails and left-skewness. It is possible to calculate VaR without assuming normality and this is the approach employed by the historical method. This involves finding the lowest returns in the real historical data. To calculate VaR at the 1% (98%, two-tailed)

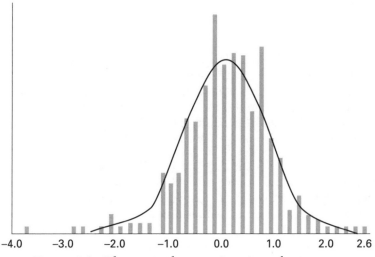

Figure 4.6 The normal approximation of returns..

probability level we need to rank the daily returns and identify the lowest 1% of returns. The first percentile (i.e., the first 1%) return is found to be −1.73%. This gives us a daily VaR of:

$$\frac{1.73}{100} \times 110 \times £500 = £951.50$$

This is almost 23% greater than the VaR estimate using the analytical method.

If we wish to recalculate the VaR for a different holding period, without making the assumption of serial independence, we cannot simply multiply the 1-day VaR by the square root of the time involved. Instead, we have to recalculate all returns for the new holding period (i.e., the weekly returns over a year, say), construct the new frequency distribution and identify the value for the appropriate percentile ranges.

SIMULATION METHODOLOGY

It may not be appropriate to calculate VaR directly by establishing the probability distribution of returns on the instrument itself, as we did for the long gilt future. This occurs because:

- for a large or complex portfolio it is impossible or impractical to maintain historical data on all the instruments involved;
- historical data are unavailable for many instruments, especially customised ones.

In such cases the historic dataset used to calculate VaR will consist of returns not on the instruments themselves, but on their 'risk factors'. There are other instruments or factors that influence their values. For example, for a domestic bond the risk factor is the interest rate; and for equity derivatives the risk factor is the value of the related index, such as the FTSE 100.

In such cases we can improve on the pure historical approach by using 'historic simulation'. Instead of looking at the volatility of actual portfolio returns in the past we can simulate the past portfolio returns by using the actual values of the risk factors and the current portfolio composition. We then construct the frequency distribution of the simulated portfolio returns by ranking them into percentiles and determining the VaR at the chosen confidence level.

Volatility over time

By calculating the volatility of daily returns we assume that this volatility is constant throughout the year. Of course, volatility can and does change over time and it may make sense to give more weight to recent observations in forecasting future volatility.

In our example, had we used only the last two months of returns rather that a full year, we would have found the standard deviation to be 0.6513 rather than 0.605 074. This would have resulted in a VaR of £834.63, rather than £775.5, as shown below:

$$0.6513 \times 2.33 = 1.5175$$

$$= \frac{1.5175}{100} \times 110 \times £500$$

$$= £834.63$$

One way to estimate volatility is through exponential weighting of observations. This emphasises more recent observations at the expense of more distant ones, because the weights attached to past observations decline over time. The volatilities and correlations are updated every day in accordance with the most recent data, as the earliest observation is dropped from the historical series and the newest ones are added.

The formula for the standard deviation (σ) of the daily return (R) and mean return (m) with exponential weights based on a historical period of N days is given as:

$$\sigma = \sqrt{(1 - \lambda) \sum_{i=1}^{N} \lambda^i (R_{N-i} - \mu)^2}$$

The parameter λ is known as the decay factor; it determines how fast the weight on past observations decays. The higher the λ, the slower is the rate of decay and the more weight is given to the more distant observations. This would have the effect of reducing the VaR in our example.

Application

Using decay factors enables us to incorporate recent trends in volatility. If volatility has recently been trending higher, the portfolio

VaR is higher if a decay factor is used at all (higher decay then reduces this number).

Not using a decay factor has the disadvantage of failing to account fully for recent changes in volatility but the advantage of being more stable and less vulnerable to irregularities in a few recent returns.

It is advisable to reduce the decay factor after a significant market correction or crash; otherwise, a risk report will place excessive reliance on recent high volatility, which would be likely to reduce following a downward correction.

The RiskMetrics dataset incorporates a fixed decay factor of 6%, meaning that each day's volatility only counts as 94% the day after. Bloomberg offers a VaR system on its terminal based on Risk-Metrics but with the option of setting a decay factor of between 0% and 9%.

BLOOMBERG SCREENS

Bloomberg users can use the screen PVAR to calculate the 1-year VaR for a bond portfolio. The portfolio must be set up first. For illustration we set up an hypothetical portfolio comprised of the following securities:

- £10 million nominal UK Treasury 5% 2014;
- £10 million nominal UK Treasury 5% 2012;
- £10 million cash.

The portfolio is shown at Figure 4.7, which is the portfolio page obtained as part of the menu for the PVAR page. This shows the market value of each of the securities; the market value of the cash is of course unchanged (the 'price' of 1.737 is the USD/GBP exchange rate). The total market value as at 28 December 2005 is £31,373,392. The VaR for each portfolio component is shown alongside.

The actual 1-year VaR is shown at Figure 4.8. This is part of the PVAR screen menu, obtained by running RPT <go>. We see that the VaR for differing probability of loss figures is given. The highlighted 5% value reflects the fact that a 95% c.i. is the most commonly calculated number.

The last exhibit, Figure 4.9, shows the one-currency VaR, in this case in pounds sterling.

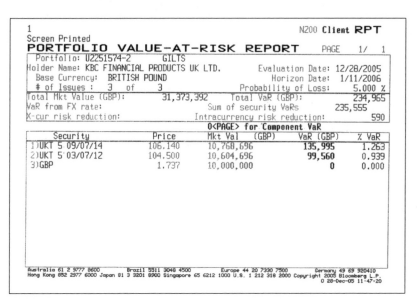

Figure 4.7 Hypothetical gilt portfolio set up on Bloomberg, as of 28 December 2005.

© Bloomberg L.P. Used with permission. Visit *www.bloomberg.com*

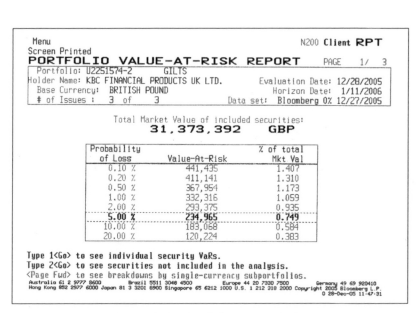

Figure 4.8 Portfolio 1-year VaR.

© Bloomberg L.P. Used with permission. Visit *www.bloomberg.com*

```
Page                                          N200 Client RPT

PORTFOLIO  VALUE-AT-RISK  REPORT      PAGE    2/   3
  Portfolio: U2251574-2      GILTS
Holder Name: KBC FINANCIAL PRODUCTS UK LTD.      Evaluation Date: 12/28/2005
  Base Currency:  BRITISH POUND                     Horizon Date:  1/11/2006
  # of Issues :   3  of    3              Probability of Loss:     5.000 %
  Total VaR :            234,965  Sum of currency-specific VaRs:       234,965
  VaR from exchange rate risk:        Percent of total value: -0.000%


                        # of  1-crncy VaR  % @ risk  % @ risk     Sector
        Currency        Secs     (GBP)     of Curr   of Port.   Value (GBP)
  1)  BRITISH POUND       3     234,965    0.749     0.749      31,373,392
```

Australia 61 2 9777 8600   Brazil 5511 3048 4500   Europe 44 20 7330 7500   Germany 49 69 920410
Hong Kong 852 2977 6000 Japan 81 3 3201 8900 Singapore 65 6212 1000 U.S. 1 212 318 2000 Copyright 2005 Bloomberg L.P.
                                                                      O 28-Dec-05 11:47:37

Figure 4.9   Portfolio one-currency VaR.

© Bloomberg L.P. Used with permission. Visit *www.bloomberg.com*

Chapter

5

. . . .

OPTIONS: RISK AND VALUE-AT-RISK

It was the increasing use of trading instruments exhibiting non-linear characteristics such as options that was the prime mover behind the development and adoption of value-at-risk type methodologies, as traditional risk measures such as modified duration were deemed to be less and less adequate. This chapter introduces the application of VaR to option instruments. First though, we look at the Black–Scholes option pricing model (*B-S model*).

OPTION VALUATION USING THE BLACK–SCHOLES MODEL

We begin with a brief overview of the valuation of options. For a basic description of options we recommend *Financial Market Analysis* by David Blake, while Robert Kolb's *Futures, Options and Swaps* provides a good description of the B-S model.

Option pricing

The original valuation model, and still commonly used in the market for plain vanilla options, was the Black–Scholes model (*B-S*), which was first presented by its authors in 1973. The basic model is:

$$C = SN(\text{d}1) - e^{-rt}XN(\text{d}2) \qquad (5.1)$$

where

$$\text{d}1 = \frac{\ln\left(\frac{S}{X}\right) + \left(r + \frac{\sigma^2}{2}\right)t}{\sigma\sqrt{t}}$$

$$\text{d}2 = \text{d}1 - \sigma\sqrt{t}$$

and

C   is the price of a call option;
S   is the current price of the underlying asset;
X   is the strike price;
r   is the risk-free interest rate;
t   is the time to expiry;
$N(\cdot)$ is the cumulative normal distribution function;
σ is the volatility of the underlying asset returns.

The expression $N(\text{d}1)$ uses the normal distribution to calculate the *delta* of the option, while $N(\text{d}2)$ calculates the probability that the option will be exercised.

The B-S model provides a single formula to enable the fair price of a call option (and through the put–call parity theorem, a put option as well) to be calculated. The formula can be interpreted as measuring the expected present value of an option based on the key assumption that prices follow a log-normal distribution. Note that deriving the B-S model involves some frightening mathematics and so will not be shown here!

For the valuation of a plain vanilla European call option, it is quite easy to set up a B-S calculation using Microsoft Excel. Consider the following call option details:

Underlying asset price	£20
Volatility	10.00%
Time to maturity	3 months
Strike price	£18
Interest rate	5.00%

The Excel calculation and cell formulae are given in Table 5.1. The price of the call option, which is in-the-money, is £2.23. The *delta* of the option is given by $N(d1)$ and in the example is 0.99. It is related to the probability that the option will be exercised. The delta value is important with respect to the hedge that the option trader puts on for the option position.

Table 5.1 Call option valuation using B-S model and Microsoft Excel.

Cell	E	F	H	I	
D7	Option parameters				Cell formulas
8	Asset price	20	ln (S/X)	0.105361	=LN(F8/F11)
9	Volatility	0.1	Adjusted return	0.01125	=(F12-F9^2/2)*F10
10	Time to expiry	0.25	Time adjusted vol	0.05	=F9*F10^0.5
11	Exercise price	18	d2	2.33221	=(I8+I9)/I10
12	Interest rate	0.05	N(d2)	0.990155	=NORMSDIST(I11)
13					
14					
15			d1	2.38221	=I11+I10
16			N(d1)	0.991395	=NORMSDIST(I15)
17					
18			Discount factor	0.987578	=EXP(-F10*F12)
19					
20			Call price	2.226514	=+F8*I16-F11*I12*I18

Volatility

Of the inputs to the B-S model, the variability of the underlying asset, or its volatility, is the most problematic. The distribution of asset prices is assumed to follow a log-normal distribution, because the logarithm of the prices is normally distributed (we assume log-normal rather than normal distribution to allow for the fact that prices cannot – as could be the case in a normal distribution – have negative values): the range of possible prices starts at 0 and cannot assume a negative value. Returns are defined as the logarithm of the price relatives and are assumed to follow the normal distribution such that:

$$\ln\left(\frac{S_t}{S_0}\right) \sim N(\mu t, \sigma\sqrt{t}) \qquad (5.2)$$

where $\quad S_0 =$ Price at time 0;

$S_t =$ Price at time t;

$N(m, s) =$ Random variable with both mean and standard deviation;

$\mu =$ Annual rate of return;

$\sigma =$ Annualised standard deviation of returns;

and the symbol $\sim$ means 'is distributed according to'.

Volatility is defined in the equation above as the annualised standard deviation of returns (prices). Price relatives are calculated from the ratio of successive closing prices. Returns are then calculated according to the following equation as the logarithm of the price relatives:

$$\text{Return} = \ln\left(\frac{S_{t+1}}{S_t}\right) \qquad (5.3)$$

where $\quad S_t =$ Market price at time t;

$S_{t+1} =$ Price one period later.

The mean and standard deviation of returns follow standard statistical techniques using the following formula:

$$\mu = \sum_{i=I}^{N} \frac{x_i}{N} \quad \text{and} \quad \sigma = \sqrt{\sum_{i=I}^{N} \frac{(x - \mu)^2}{N - 1}} \qquad (5.4)$$

where $\quad x_i = i$th price relative;

$N =$ Total number of observations.

This gives a standard deviation or volatility of daily price returns. To convert this to an annual figure, it is necessary to multiply it by the

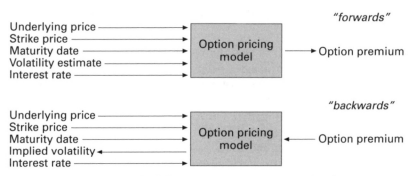

Figure 5.1   Model pricing and implied volatility.

square root of the number of working days in a year, normally taken to be 250.

Calculations such as these produce a figure for *historic volatility*. What is required is a figure for *future* volatility, since this is relevant for pricing an option expiring in the future. Future volatility cannot be measured directly, by definition. Market-makers get around this by using an option pricing model 'backwards', as shown in Figure 5.1.

An option pricing model calculates the option price from volatility and other parameters. Used in reverse the model can calculate the volatility implied by the option price. Volatility measured in this way is called *implied volatility*. Evaluating implied volatility is straightforward using this method and generally more appropriate than using historic volatility.

THE GREEKS

As we noted in the previous section the price of an option depends on five variables. Of these the strike price is normally (but not always) fixed in advance. This leaves four variables. Option traders follow a number of quantities, each of which measures how the price of an option will change when one of the input parameters changes while the others remain unchanged. The measures are identified by letters from ancient Greek and so are known as the 'Greeks'; the main ones are summarised below.

Delta

The delta of an option is the change in premium (price) for a unit change in the underlying asset price. In the B-S model it is given by $N(d1)$. It is the main measure of market risk, and its value drives the hedge. The premise behind the B-S model concept is that of the 'risk-neutral' portfolio that mirrors the option. The size of this risk-neutral portfolio is given by the delta. So, for example, from Table 5.1 we see that the delta is 0.991. This means that if the underlying asset goes up in price from £20 to £21, the value of the option will go up by £0.991. Therefore, if an options trader sells 1,000 call options on the underlying security, his delta-neutral portfolio will be long 991 of the security.

We saw how the delta was calculated in Table 5.1.

Gamma

Gamma is like the convexity of a bond, it is a measure of the rate of change of delta. That is, it is the change in *delta* for a unit change in the underlying asset price. Gamma is given by:

$$\Gamma = \frac{N'(d_1)}{S\sigma\sqrt{t}} \tag{5.5}$$

where the inputs are as before. The gamma of an option is always negative for the person who has written (sold) the option.

The existence of gamma means that an options portfolio must be delta-hedged on a regular basis – that is, *dynamically hedged* – because delta is always changing. The higher gamma is, the more often the hedge must be rebalanced, because it indicates a faster changing delta.

Table 5.2 illustrates calculation of gamma, using the same option parameters as Table 5.1, except we change the current underlying price from 20 to 21. This is to demonstrate the gamma value, which was almost identical to the value for $N'(d1)$ at the price of 20 and may have confused readers. As before, we show the Excel formulae so that students can construct the spreadsheet themselves. Note we set *pi* with a value of 3.1416.

A value of 0.001 352 423 means that if the asset price increases by 1 (i.e., from 21 to 22) then the delta will increase by 0.001 35.

Table 5.2   Option gamma and Excel formula.

Cell	E	F	H	I	J	K
D7	**Option parameters**					**Cell formulas**
8	Asset price S	21	ln (S/X)	0.15415068		=LN(F8/F11)
9	Volatility	0.1	Adjusted return	0.01125		=(F12-F9^2/2)*F10
10	Time to expiry	0.25	Time adjusted vol	0.05		=F9*F10^0.5
11	Exercise price X	18	d2	3.308013597		=(I8+I9)/I10
12	Interest rate	0.05	N(d2)	0.999530141		=NORMSDIST(I11)
13			d1	3.358013597		=I11+I10
14			N(d1)	0.999607422		=NORMSDIST(I13)
15						
16			Coefficient	0.398941814		=(2*3.1416)^-0.5
17			(d1^2/2)	5.638127657		=I13^2/2
18			Exp-(d1^2/2)	0.003559527		=EXP(-I17)
19			N'(d1)	0.001420044		=I16*I18
20						
21			Gamma	0.001352423		=I19/(F8*I10)

Option gamma, like delta, is at its highest for at-the-money options and will decrease as the option becomes in-the-money or out-of-the-money. Gamma exposure is not captured by some VaR measurement methods, and risk managers must therefore gamma-adjust their calculations. Any calculation for gamma, like that for convexity, is always an approximation and is a dynamic, not static, number.

Vega

Vega is the change in option premium for a unit change in volatility (usually 1%) of the underlying security. It is sometimes called *kappa*. Vega is given by:

$$Vega = S\sqrt{\Delta t}N(d1) \tag{5.6}$$

The term $N(d1)$ is the equation for the normal distribution, which is given by:

$$N(x) = \frac{1}{\sqrt{2\Pi}}e^{-x2/2} \tag{5.7}$$

Table 5.3 illustrates calculation of vega for the same option seen in Table 5.1.

The vega value of 0.234 means that a 1% increase in volatility in the underlying security will produce a 0.234 increase in option premium. Similarly with gamma, vega sensitivity is most acute when the option is at-the-money. Option value increases with volatility, so being long vega is attractive to a trader if he is running a long position.

Table 5.3   Option vega.

Cell	E	F	H	I	J	K
D7	**Option parameters**					**Cell formulas**
8	Asset price	20	ln (S/X)	0.10536052		=LN(F8/F11)
9	Volatility	10.00%	Adjusted return	0.01125		=(F12-F9^2/2)*F10
10	Time to expiry	0.25	Time adjusted vol	0.05		=F9*F10^0.5
11	Exercise price	18	d2	2.33221031		=(I8+I9)/I10
12	Interest rate	0.05	N(d2)	0.99015521		=NORMSDIST(I11)
13			d1	2.38221031		=I11+I10
14			N(d1)	0.99139548		=NORMSDIST(I13)
15						
16			Coefficient	0.39894181		=(2*3.1416)^-0.5
17			(d1^2/2)	2.83746299		=I13^2/2
18			Exp-(d1^2/2)	0.05857408		=EXP(-I17)
19			N'(d1)	0.02336765		=I16*I18
20						
21			Vega	0.2336765		=F8*F10^0.5*I19

Other greeks

The other Greeks include:

Theta   The change in the premium for a unit change in the time to expiry (usually 1 day).

Rho   The change in premium for a unit change in interest rates (usually 1%).

Lambda   The percentage change in premium for a percentage change in the underlying asset price.

RISK MEASUREMENT

As well as using a VaR estimate, option trading desks employ a range of further risk measurement tools. We highlight some of these below.

Spot ladder

This report shows the portfolio value and Greeks for a ladder of values of the underlying asset (it is also known as an asset ladder). It facilitates analysis of a position affected by large market moves. The report measures the sensitivity of the portfolio to changes in the underlying cash market prices.

Maturity ladder

A report showing portfolio Greeks broken down into maturity buckets, measuring the maturity profile from 1 day out to expiry of the longest dated position. It is used to ensure that hedges are adapted to the expiry profile of the portfolio.

Across-time ladder

A report displaying spot ladder values for a range of future dates. It shows how the portfolio value changes as it matures (all else being equal). This enables traders to check whether the hedge is still effective over time.

Jump risk

Derivatives desks often produce reports for trading books showing the effect on portfolio value of a 1-bp move, along each part of the term structure of interest rates. For example, such a report would show that a change of 1 basis point in 3-month rates would result in a change in value of £x – this measure is often referred to as a price variation per basis point, or sometimes as present value of a basis point ($PVBP$).

Jump risk refers to the effect on value of an upward move of 100 basis points for all interest rates – that is, for all points of the term structure. The jump risk figure is therefore the change in the value of the portfolio for a 1% parallel shift in the yield curve.

Table 5.4 shows an extract from a risk report with the PVBP for selected points along the term structure. The jump risk report will show the effect of a 1% interest rate move across all grid points; the sum of all the value changes is the jump risk.

Table 5.5 shows an extract from the jump risk report for a currency options book of a major investment bank.

APPLYING VaR FOR OPTIONS

For a risk manager a portfolio's market risk may be quantified as a single VaR number; however, management of individual trading books often requires more data to understand risk sensitivities than

Table 5.4   PVBP per grid point:
extract from risk report.

Grid point (days)	PVBP (£)
1	1
7	5
91	−1,658
183	928
365	500
730	−1,839
1,643	−944
3,650	1,365
7,300	0
9,125	0

Table 5.5   Jump risk report.

	Limits	Total VaR	Jump risk
AUD	3,500	1,312	−9,674
CHF	1,750	663	−7,802
DEM	5,000	3,969	−57,246
GBP	7,500	5,695	−74,215
JPY	150,000	49,563	−536,199
USD	4,500	3,339	−33,289
Total	172,250	64,541	−718,425

are provided by VaR alone. This is particularly true for options, where the effect of sensitivity to the Greeks can be significant. The behaviour of options calls for some fine-tuning in applying VaR.

The standard assumption made by most VaR models is that returns (prices) are normally distributed. This allows VaR to be estimated. Returns, in fact, are not distributed normally in practice. Market crashes are more common in the real world than suggested by the normal distribution; it is this factor that calls for the use of stress-testing and scenario analysis. The returns on an option portfolio are also not usually normally distributed. Option instruments have a non-linear pay-out profile. This means that the relationship between a change in the underlying asset price and the resulting change in the option price is not constant. We have already referred to this relationship as the option's delta.

Consider an at-the-money call option on an equity index, which is initially set at a level of 1,020 points. If the index value drops by 10 points to 1,010, the value of the option decreases by roughly 5 points because it has about an equal chance of expiring in-the-money or out-of-the-money. But if the index drops a further 10 points to 1,000, the value of the option may drop by just 3 points, even though the index has moved the same amount as before. This is an example of non-linearity: the option delta is 50% when the index is at 1,020, but has changed to 30% when the index is at 1,010. The relationship between delta and the value of the underlying is the *gamma*. Non-linearity becomes more important as the option becomes more in-the-money and as it approaches expiry.

VaR models allow for delta, which is the linear component of option risk. This allows assumption of the normal distribution, despite inaccuracies. However, for banks running large option books with exposure to significant gamma risk these inaccuracies cannot be ignored. Option prices also are sensitive to the time remaining to expiry (theta) and the underlying volatility (vega). In addition, the Basel CAD II rules will stipulate that banks which write options must measure delta, gamma and vega risk when calculating capital to be held against them.

If the effects of gamma risk are introduced when calculating the potential returns in a portfolio, the distribution of returns becomes asymmetric, or skewed, as shown in Figure 5.2.

Other variables such as mean and variance may also differ from a normal distribution. The statistical measures that describe the normal distribution therefore do not apply. The solution to this is to include the effects of higher order risk sensitivities, such as gamma. The portfolio VaR can then be calculated on the basis of this skewed distribution. There are three alternatives:

- the skewed distribution can be approximated to a deformed normal distribution;
- the 5th and 95th percentiles can be calculated for the skewed distribution;

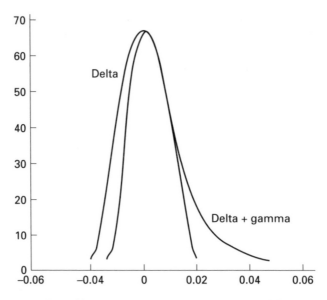

Figure 5.2 The effect of incorporating gamma risk on portfolio distributions.

- the skewed distribution can be fitted to a more general family of distributions whose statistical measures are known.

However, an analytic approximation to VaR ignores some of the elements which make up the market risk of the portfolio, including the effects of gamma and market crashes. To capture these effects requires other approaches, such as Monte Carlo or historical simulation.

Banks prefer simulation for the reasons mentioned above. The only drawback with simulation, given the large number of trials that are required, is that it is time-consuming and requires considerable computing power. There is, therefore, a trade-off between accuracy and speed of calculation.

Example 5.1 Option VaR.

Call option on £10 million March 1998 long gilt future:

Data on option

Price	= 2.938
Estimated delta (for change in yield)	= −380.2
Estimated gamma (for change in yield)	= 26,440
Estimated vega	= 14.95
(for change in volatility of yield)	

Risk calculations

(a) Market value of position		= £293,800
(b) The 98% daily VaR is		= £72,500,
		derived as follows:

	Delta risk	= £75,000
less	Convexity risk	= −£5,000
plus	Volatility risk	= £2,500
equals	Value-at-risk	= £72,500

The gamma effect on the distribution curve is illustrated in Figure 5.3. For a long position the gamma position is always positive, so the distribution is shifted to the right.

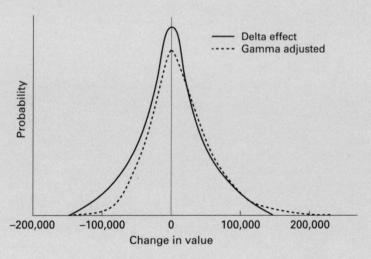

Figure 5.3 Gamma-adjusted VaR calculation.

Chapter

6

....

MONTE CARLO SIMULATION AND VALUE-AT-RISK

A defining characteristic of options is their non-linear pay-off profile. This makes risk exposure estimation for an options portfolio more problematic compared with a portfolio comprised of linear pay-off profile instruments such as bonds, futures and swaps. For this reason practitioners frequently eschew the variance–covariance methodology in favour of what is called the Monte Carlo simulation approach, because it is believed to provide a more accurate estimation of risk exposure for option instruments. Monte Carlo simulation refers to a process whereby a series of prices for an asset (or assets) is generated by a computer program; these prices are all theoretically possible given certain user-specified parameters. The portfolio is then revalued at each of these possible prices, and this enables the user to calculate a VaR number for the portfolio.

In this chapter we introduce the Monte Carlo simulation method and its use as a value-at-risk (VaR) calculation methodology.

INTRODUCTION: MONTE CARLO SIMULATION

We first consider the concept of simulated prices and their application to option valuation.

Option value under Monte Carlo

Table 6.1 reprises our European option contract from Chapter 5. Note an additional parameter, the 'drift'. This reflects what is known as the stochastic nature of asset price movements as defined in the Black–Scholes model (B-S model); a stochastic movement is described by volatility and drift. The drift is the measure of how much the price movement moves back around a mean figure.

Assume we have run a simulation program or a random number generator, and from ten such numbers we have derived ten possible future asset prices. The series of ten asset prices is shown in Column H in Table 6.1. On expiry the option is seen to have positive value in eight of the cases; this is given in Column J. Where the option expires out-of-the-money it, of course, carries zero value and would not be exercised. Any positive value is realised on expiry, which is in the future, so we discount the pay-out to obtain a value for the option today. These values are shown in Column K. The discount factor used is the same as that seen in Table 5.1 (p. 89).

Table 6.1 Option valuation following Monte Carlo simulation.

Cell	E	F	G H	I	J	K
			Simulation results		**Option intrinsic value**	**Option present value**
D7	**Option parameters**					
8	Asset price	20		1	26.3	8.3	8.19690
9	Volatility	10.00%		2	21.2	3.2	3.16025
10	Time to expiry	0.25		3	16.4	0	0.00000
11	Exercise price	18		4	13.8	0	0.00000
12	Interest rate	0.05		5	28.2	10.2	10.07329
13	Drift	6%		6	24.5	6.5	6.41926
14				7	23.7	5.7	5.62919
15	Discount factor	0.9875778		8	18.9	0.9	0.88882
16				9	21.4	3.4	3.35776
17	Average value (option value)	4.52311		10	25.6	7.6	7.50559
18						
19						
20						

Table 6.2 Spreadsheet formulae for Table 6.1.

Cell	E	F	G	H	I	J	K
				Simulation results		**Option intrinsic value**	**Option present value**
D7	**Option parameters**						
8	Asset price	20		1	26.3	=MAX(G8-D11,0)	=H8*D15
9	Volatility	10.00%		2	21.2	=MAX(G9-D11,0)	=H9*D15
10	Time to expiry	0.25		3	16.4	=MAX(G10-D11,0)	=H10*D15
11	Exercise price	18		4	13.8	=MAX(G11-D11,0)	=H11*D15
12	Interest rate	0.05		5	28.2	=MAX(G12-D11,0)	=H12*D15
13	Drift	6%		6	24.5	=MAX(G13-D11,0)	=H13*D15
14				7	23.7	=MAX(G14-D11,0)	=H14*D15
15	Discount factor	=EXP(-F10*F12)		8	18.9	=MAX(G15-D11,0)	=H15*D15
16				9	21.4	=MAX(G16-D11,0)	=H16*D15
17	Average value (option value)	=AVERAGE(K8:K17)		10	25.6	=MAX(G17-D11,0)	=H17*D15
18						
19						
20						

The extent of possible values for the option then ranges from £0 to £10. To calculate the fair value we take the average of the range which gives us the theoretical price of the option. The average value is £4.52. Following the logic of the B-S model, the probability that the option will be exercised is 80%, because eight out of the ten simulated values resulted in positive value.

The spreadsheet formulae for Table 6.1 are given at Table 6.2.

Monte Carlo distribution

In practice, the parameters input to a Monte Carlo simulation are set to approximate the generated values to a normal distribution. This recognises that asset prices revert back to their mean over time; the probability that prices move very far away from the mean is remote. In other words, an asset priced at £20 and with a volatility of 10% is unlikely to be priced at £2 in 1 year's time (and equally unlikely to be priced at £40 in the same period). Note that it is the return on a security that follows the log-normal distribution, and not the prices of the security itself.

We observe this in our simulated prices at Table 6.1. The average of the series is 22, which is actually spot on with the expected value of the underlying in 1 year's time (given by the volatility value). There is a procedure to generate random figures in Excel, which was used in our example. The formulae needed for this are given in Table 6.3.

Table 6.3 Excel formulae for random number generation.

	Trial 1	Trial 2, etc.
Random number	=RAND()	
Standard deviations	=NORMSINV(E6)	
Growth	=F13+E7*F9*F10^0.5	
Exponential growth	=EXP(E8)	
Simulated share price	=F8*E9	
Option intrinsic value	=MAX(E10-F11,0)	
Discount factor	=EXP(-E11*E13)	
PV of option	=E11^E12	

Monte Carlo simulation and VaR

We noted that the pay-off profile nature of options means that most VaR calculation methodologies are unsuitable for risk exposure measurement of an option book. The Monte Carlo method is regarded as the most accurate method to use in this case, most especially for exotic options.

To apply the concept to VaR, we simply generate the random number profile and then apply a cut-off at the percentile that suits our purpose. For example, with the example above, rather than just running ten simulations we can run the program, say, 5,000 or 10,000 times and then cut off the results at the 250th or 500th lowest value – this value would represent a 95% confidence interval VaR number.

Example 6.1   Portfolio volatility using variance–covariance and simulation methods.

A simple two-asset portfolio is composed of the following instruments:

	Gilt strip	*FTSE 100 stock*
Number of units	£100 million	£5 million
Market value	£54.39 million	£54 million
Daily volatility	£0.18 million	£0.24 million

The correlation between the two assets is 20%. Using (3.1) we calculate the portfolio VaR as follows:

$$Vol = \sqrt{s_{bond}^2 + s_{stock}^2 + 2s_{bond}s_{stock}r_{bond,\,stock}}$$

$$Vol = \sqrt{0.18^2 + 0.24^2 + (2 \times 0.18 \times 0.24 \times 0.2)}$$

$$= 0.327$$

We have ignored the weighting element for each asset because the market values are roughly equal. The calculation gives a portfolio volatility of £0.327 million. For a 95% confidence level VaR measure, which corresponds to 1.645 standard deviations (in a one-tailed test) we multiply the portfolio volatility by 1.645, which gives us a portfolio VaR of £0.538 million.

In a Monte Carlo simulation we also calculate the correlation and volatilities of the portfolio. These values are used as parameters in a random number simulation to throw out changes in the underlying portfolio value. These values are used to re-price the portfolio, and this value will be either a gain or loss on the actual mark-to-market value. This process is repeated for each random number that is generated. In Table 6.4 we show the results for 15 simulations of our two-asset portfolio. From the results we read off the loss level that corresponds to the required confidence interval.

Table 6.4   Monte Carlo simulation results.

Simulation	Market value		Portfolio value	Profit/Loss
	Bond	Stock		
1	54.35	54.9	109.25	0.86
2	54.64	54.02	108.66	0.27
3	54.4	53.86	108.26	−0.13
4	54.25	54.15	108.4	0.01
5	54.4	54.17	108.57	0.18
6	54.4	54.03	108.43	0.04
7	54.31	53.84	108.15	−0.24
8	54.3	53.96	108.26	−0.13
9	54.46	54.11	108.57	0.18
10	54.32	53.92	108.24	−0.15
11	54.31	53.97	108.28	−0.11
12	54.47	54.08	108.55	0.16
13	54.38	54.03	108.41	0.02
14	54.71	53.89	108.6	0.21
15	54.29	54.05	108.34	−0.05

As the number of trials is increased, the results from a Monte Carlo simulation approach those of the variance–covariance measure. This is shown in Figure 6.1.

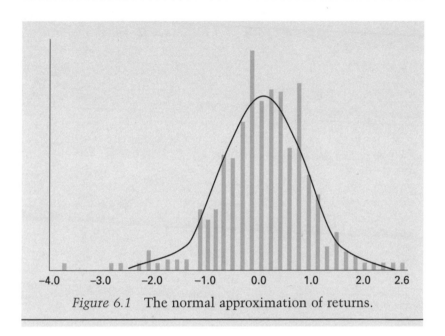

Figure 6.1 The normal approximation of returns.

Chapter

7

....

REGULATORY ISSUES AND STRESS-TESTING

W e consider briefly, and in overview manner only, some relevant issues in bank regulatory capital. We then discuss the issue of stress-testing of value-at-risk (*VaR*) models.

CAPITAL ADEQUACY

The European Union (*EU*) Capital Adequacy Directive (*CAD*) has been in place since January 1996. It defines the capital requirement calculation that banks and securities houses must comply with based on the relocation of positions between the trading book and the non-trading, or banking, book.

Model compliance

As part of complying with CAD I, the Bank of England (*BoE*) has adopted a procedure it uses to recognise models and the capital requirements which will be generated from these models. Eligible models can cover:

• options risk and interest rate risk in derivatives in the trading book;
• foreign exchange (*FX*) risk in the banking and trading books.

There is a standard approach for banks without recognised models and a more complex approach for those with recognised models, which will normally result in a lower capital requirement for a given quantity of position risk.

Models eligible for recognition fall into two categories:

• pricing models (for complex swaps, vanilla and exotic options);
• risk aggregation models (those which summarise and facilitate management of risk).

The types of risk aggregation models which the BoE can recognise for CAD purposes include VaR-type models used for the measurement of interest rate risk, position risk and FX risk.

VaR models

Banks wishing to use their own VaR model for calculating capital requirements under CAD must have it recognised by the BoE. No particular type of model is prescribed and banks may use models based on back-testing, variance–covariance matrices, Monte Carlo simulations or simple aggregation of risk numbers.

If using their own models banks must be able to calculate the CAD requirement on a date randomly chosen by the BoE supervisor, and notify the supervisor of the calculation the following day. The bank will then be required to calculate its capital requirement both according to the standard method and its own VaR model.

The model review process

The BoE model review process includes discussion of the following areas:

- the mathematics of the model and underlying assumptions;
- systems and controls;
- risk management, reporting procedures and limits;
- staffing issues;
- reconciliation and valuation procedures;
- the setting of capital requirements.

Certain conditions and standards need to be met prior to recognition of the model. These standards vary according to the size of the firm, the nature of the business and the type of model being used. The review process takes the form of an on-site visit with follow-up of any outstanding issues to be met before recognition can be granted.

CAD II

CAD II is the key EU directive that allows financial firms to use internal VaR models to calculate market risk capital requirements in line with Basel standards. This is known as the internal models approach. The directive was implemented in 1999. Firms will have the opportunity to base their market risk capital charges for all or part of their business on their internally determined VaR. To use this approach firms must meet certain qualitative and quantitative criteria to the satisfaction of their regulators.

Under both CAD II as adopted by the EU and the 1997 amendment to the Basel Accord – developed by the Bank for International Settlements (BIS) – banks can choose whether to use the standard approach to calculating capital requirements for trading books (equities, interest rate instruments, FX and commodities) or to seek supervisory approval to employ their own in-house VaR models as the basis for capital calculation.

Excessive reliance on models raises questions about necessary safeguards to ensure that the capital requirements generated are adequate. Basel addressed this in a number of ways. One was to lay down simple standards for the construction of models. The standards decreed by the BIS include:

- the model was to express a VaR estimate to a 99% degree of confidence;
- losses must be calculated on the basis of a 10-day holding period;
- historic data must cover at least the last 12 months.

The BIS does not prescribe the *type* of model to be used. An additional requirement from Basel includes a requirement for banks to hold the higher of (i) the VaR number suggested by the model or (ii) three times the 60-day moving average of the VaR numbers generated on the current and past trading books.

Quantitative requirements

BIS guidelines have been adopted by national regulatory authorities. The SFA – later integrated into the Financial Services Authority (*FSA*) – in *Board Notice 458*, February 1998, set out requirements to form part of model recognition in the UK. A daily VaR number should be calculated using:

- a 99% one-tailed confidence interval;
- a 10-day holding period;
- a historical observation period of 1 year, except where a significant increase in volatility may justify a shorter period;
- datasets updated on a frequent basis (at least every 3 months).

These requirements are based on the BIS guidelines.

Risk factors

Financial firms must be able to identify appropriate risk factors that capture the risks of a portfolio. CAD II requires that the following factors be modelled:

- interest rate risk; the yield curve should be divided into a minimum number of six maturity segments;
- FX risk;

- equity risk;
- commodity risk;
- correlations.

Qualitative requirements

CAD II will impose certain qualitative criteria that firms must satisfy if using their internal models for regulatory purposes. These include that:

- the risk model be closely integrated into the daily risk management processes of the firm;
- the firm has an independent risk control unit ('middle office', etc.);
- the firm has sufficient staff skilled in the use of sophisticated models;
- the firm has established procedures for the risk management function;
- the firm frequently conducts a programme of stress-testing.

Specific risk

This is the risk of a price change in an instrument due to factors relating to its issuer or, for a derivative, the issuer of the underlying.

Regulatory capital requirement

A firm's market risk capital charge will be calculated as the higher of a multiple of the previous day's VaR and a multiple of the average of the VaR estimated on each of the preceding 60 business days.

The financial resources requirement element of this can be stated using the following expression:

$$FRR_{VaR} = \text{Max}\left(f_1 \times VaR_t, f_2 \times \frac{1}{60}\sum_{i=0}^{59} VaR_{t-i}\right) + SR$$

where
VaR_t = Previous day's VaR number;
VaR_{t-i} = VaR calculated i business days earlier;
f_1, f_2 = Multiplicative factors;
SR = Specific risk add-on.

CAD II requires that f_2 has a minimum value of 3 (f_1 will have a minimum value of 1). Firms are required to carry out back-testing to measure performance and if concerns arise about the accuracy or integrity of the model, the multiplicative factors can be increased by the regulator. FRR_{VaR} will be added under a standard method to obtain the firm's total capital requirement.

Back-testing

This is the process of comparing VaR risk estimates to actual portfolio performance. For each business day firms should compare the 1-day VaR measure calculated by their model and the actual 1-day change in the portfolio value. For each actual loss greater than predicted, an 'exception' (see below) is reported. For multiple exceptions a plus factor of between 0 and 1 is applied to the firm's f_2 multiplicative factor.

The BIS and central bank supervisors carry out back-testing as a check on the accuracy of the models, by comparing actual trading results with model-generated risk measures. This has posed problems because trading results are often affected by changes to portfolios in the period following calculation of the initial VaR estimate. For this reason the BIS has recommended that banks develop their own capability to perform back-testing. Firms that do not meet the Basel back-testing criterion for accuracy suffer additional capital charges. These charges are imposed if, over a 12-month period (250 trading days), a bank's VaR model under-predicts the number of losses exceeding the permitted 1% cut-off point. Such losses are termed 'exceptions'. If a bank's VaR model has generated 0–4 exceptions, it is said to be in the 'green zone'; for 5–9 exceptions the bank is in the 'yellow zone'; and if there are 10 or more exceptions it is in the 'red zone'. The capital requirements for banks whose models are in the yellow zone may be increased by regulators; if they are in the red zone the requirements will almost certainly be increased.

STRESS-TESTING

Risk measurement models and their associated assumptions are not without limitation. It is important to understand what will happen should some of the model's underlying assumptions break down. 'Stress-testing' is the term used for doing a series of scenario analyses or simulations to investigate the effect of extreme market conditions and/or the effect of violating any of the basic assumptions behind the risk model. If carried out efficiently, stress-testing will provide clearer information on the potential exposures at risk due to significant market corrections; hence, it is recommended practice for financial institutions.

Simulating stress

There is no standard way to do stress-testing. It is a means of experimenting with the limits of a model; it is also a means to measure the residual risk which is not effectively captured by the formal risk model, thus complementing the VaR framework. If a bank uses a confidence interval of 99% when calculating its VaR the losses on its trading portfolio due to market movements should not exceed the VaR number on more than 1 day in 100. For a 95% confidence level the corresponding frequency is 1 day in 20 or roughly 1 trading day each month. The question to ask is 'what are the expected losses on those days?' Also ,what can an institution do to protect itself against these losses? Assuming that returns are normally distributed provides a workable daily approximation for estimating risk, but when market moves are more extreme these assumptions no longer add value.

The 1% of market moves that are not used for VaR calculations contain events such as the October 1987 crash, the bond market collapse of February 1994 and the Mexican peso crisis at the end of 1994. In these cases market moves were much larger than any VaR model could account for; the correlation between markets also increased well above levels normally assumed in models. Figure 7.1 shows how actual distributions differ from the theoretical normal distribution.

An approach used by risk managers is to simulate extreme market moves over a range of different scenarios. One method is to use Monte Carlo simulation. This allows dealers to push the risk factors to greater limits; for example, a 99% confidence interval captures events up to 2.33 standard deviations from the mean asset return level. A risk manager can calculate the effect on the trading portfolio of a 10 standard deviations move. The 1987 crash was a 20 standard deviations move. Similarly, risk managers may want to change the correlation assumptions under which they normally work. For instance, if markets all move down together – something that happened in Asian markets from the end of 1997 and emerging markets

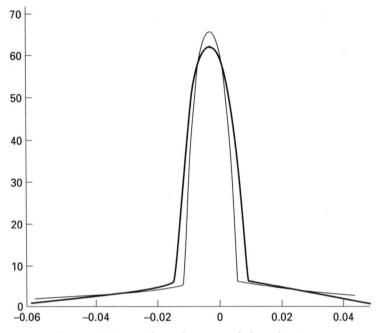

Figure 7.1   Real vs theoretical distributions.

generally from July 1998 – losses will be greater than if some markets are offset by other negatively correlated markets.

Only by pushing the bounds of the range of market moves that are covered in the stress-testing process can financial institutions have an improved chance of identifying where losses might occur, and therefore a better chance of managing their risk effectively.

Stress-testing in practice

For effective stress-testing one has to consider non-standard situations. The BIS Policy Group has recommended certain minimum standards in respect of specified market movements; the parameters chosen are considered large moves to overnight marks, including:

- parallel yield curve shifts of 100 basis points up and down;
- steepening and flattening of the yield curve (2-year to 10-year) by 25 basis points;
- increase and decrease in 3-month yield volatilities by 20%;
- increase and decrease in equity index values by 10%;
- increase and decrease in swap spread by 20 basis points.

These scenarios represent a starting point for a framework for routine stress-testing.

Banks agree that stress-testing must be used to supplement VaR models. The main problem appears to be difficulty in designing appropriate tests. The main issues are:

- difficulty in 'anticipating the unanticipated';
- adopting a systematic approach, with stress-testing carried out by looking at past extremes and analysing the effect on the VaR number under these circumstances;
- selecting ten scenarios based on past extreme events and generating portfolio VaRs based on re-runs of these scenarios.

Issues in stress-testing

Back-testing

It is to be expected that extreme market moves will not be captured in VaR measurements. The calculations will always assume that the probability of events – such as the Mexican peso devaluation – are extremely low when analysing historical or expected movements of the currency. Stress tests need to be designed to model for such occurrences. *Back-testing* a firm's qualitative and quantitative risk management approach for actual extreme events often reveals the need to adjust reserves, increase the VaR factor, adopt additional limits and controls and expand risk calculations. With back-testing a firm will take, say, its daily VaR number, which we will assume is computed to a 95% degree of confidence. The estimate will be compared with the actual trading losses suffered by the book over a 20-day period, and if there is a significant discrepancy the firm will need to go back to its model and make adjustments to parameters. Frequent and regular back-testing of the VaR model's output with actual trading losses is an important part of stress-testing.

Procedure

The procedure for stress-testing in banks usually involves:

- creation of hypothetical extreme scenarios; and
- computation of corresponding hypothetical profit and loss (*p&l*) statements.

One method is to imagine *global* scenarios. If one hypothesis is that the euro appreciates sharply against the dollar, the scenario needs to consider any related areas, such as the effect, if any, on the Japanese yen and interest rates generally.

Another method is to generate many *local* scenarios and so consider a few risk factors at a time. For example, given an FX option portfolio a bank might compute the hypothetical p&l for each currency pair under a variety of exchange rate and implied volatility scenarios. There is then the issue of amalgamating the results: one way would be to add the worst case results for each of the sub-portfolios, but this ignores any portfolio effect and cross-hedging. This may result in an over-estimate that is of little use in practice.

Chapter

8

....

CREDIT RISK AND CREDIT VALUE-AT-RISK

C redit risk emerged as a significant risk management issue in the 1990s. In increasingly competitive markets, banks and securities houses are taking on more forms of credit risk. The following are instances:

- credit spreads tightened in the late 1990s and the early part of 2000 to the point where blue chip companies – such as BT or Shell – benefitted from syndicated loans for as little as 10–12 basis points over the London Interbank Offered Rate (*Libor*); banks are turning to lower rated firms to maintain margin;
- growth in complex financial instruments that are more challenging to manage than traditional instruments, such as credit derivatives;
- investors are finding fewer opportunities in interest rate and currency markets and moving towards yield enhancement through extending and trading credit; for example, after EMU, participating government bond markets become credit markets;
- high yield (junk) and emerging market sectors have been expanding rapidly.

The growth in credit exposures and rise of complex instruments have led to a need for more sophisticated risk management techniques.

TYPES OF CREDIT RISK

There are two main types of credit risk:

- credit spread risk;
- credit default risk.

Credit spread risk

Credit spread is the excess premium required by the market for taking on a certain assumed credit exposure. Credit spread risk is the risk of financial loss resulting from changes in the level of credit spreads used in the marking-to-market of a product. It is exhibited by a portfolio for which the credit spread is traded and marked. Changes in observed credit spreads affect the value of the portfolio.

Credit default risk

This is the risk that an issuer of debt (obligor) is unable to meet its financial obligations. Where an obligor defaults, a firm generally incurs a loss equal to the amount owed by the obligor less any recovery amount which the firm recovers as a result of foreclosure, liquidation or restructuring of the defaulted obligor. All portfolios of exposures exhibit credit default risk.

CREDIT RATINGS

The risks associated with holding a fixed interest debt instrument are closely connected with the ability of the issuer to maintain the regular coupon payments as well as redeem the debt on maturity. Essentially, *credit risk* is the main risk of holding a bond. Only the highest quality government debt, and a small amount of supra-national and corporate debt, may be considered to be entirely free of credit risk. Therefore, at any time, the yield on a bond reflects investors' views on the ability of the issuer to meet its liabilities as set out in the bond's terms and conditions. A delay in paying a cash liability as it becomes due is known as technical default and is a cause for extreme concern for investors; failure to pay will result in the matter being placed in the hands of a court as investors seek to recover their funds.

Credit ratings

A credit rating is a formal opinion given by a rating agency of the *credit risk* for investors in a particular issue of debt securities. Ratings are given to public issues of debt securities by any type of entity, including governments, banks and corporates. They are also given to short-term debt, such as commercial paper, as well as bonds and medium-term notes.

Purpose of credit ratings

Investors in securities accept the risk that the issuer will default on coupon payments or fail to repay the principal in full on the maturity date. Generally, credit risk is greater for securities with a long maturity, as there is a longer period for the issuer potentially to default. For example, if a company issues 10-year bonds, investors cannot be certain that the company will still exist in 10 years' time. It may have failed and gone into liquidation some time before that. That said, there is also risk attached to short-dated debt securities;

indeed, there have been instances of default by issuers of commercial paper, which is a very short-term instrument.

The prospectus or offer document for an issue provides investors with some information about the issuer, so that some credit analysis can be performed on the issuer before the bonds are placed. The information in the offer documents enables investors themselves to perform their own credit analysis by studying this information before deciding whether or not to invest. Credit assessments take up time, however, and also require the specialist skills of credit analysts. Large institutional investors do in fact employ such specialists to carry out credit analysis; however, often it is too costly and time-consuming to assess every issuer in every debt market. Therefore, investors commonly employ two other methods when making a decision on the credit risk of debt securities:

- name recognition;
- formal credit ratings.

Name recognition is when the investor relies on the good name and reputation of the issuer and accepts that the issuer is of such good financial standing, or sufficient financial standing, that a default on interest and principal payments is highly unlikely. An investor may feel this way about, say, Microsoft or British Petroleum plc. However, the experience of Barings in 1995 suggested to many investors that it may not be wise to rely on name recognition alone in today's market-place. The tradition and reputation behind the Barings name allowed the bank to borrow at Libor, or occasionally at sub-Libor, interest rates in the money markets, which put it on a par with the highest quality clearing banks in terms of credit rating. However, name recognition needs to be augmented by other methods to reduce the risk against unforeseen events, as happened with Barings. Credit ratings are a formal assessment, for a given issue of debt securities, of the likelihood that the interest and principal will be paid in full and on schedule. They are increasingly used to make investment decisions about corporate or lesser developed government debt.

Formal credit ratings

Credit ratings are provided by specialist agencies. The major credit rating agencies are Standard & Poor's, Fitch, and Moody's, based in the United States. There are other agencies both in the US and other countries. On receipt of a formal request, the credit rating agencies will carry out a rating exercise on a specific issue of debt capital. The request for a rating comes from the organisation planning the issue of bonds. Although ratings are provided for the benefit of investors, the issuer must bear the cost. However, it is in the issuer's interest to request a rating as it raises the profile of the bonds, and investors may refuse to buy paper that is not accompanied by a recognised rating. Although the rating exercise involves a credit analysis of the issuer, the rating is applied to a specific debt issue. This means that in theory the credit rating is applied not to an organisation itself, but to the specific debt securities that the organisation has issued or is planning to issue. In practice, it is common for the market to refer to the creditworthiness of organisations themselves in terms of the rating of their debt. A highly rated company, such as Rabobank, is therefore referred to as a 'triple-A rated' company, although it is the bank's debt issues that are rated as triple-A.

Ratings changes over time

Ratings transition matrix

We have noted that the rating agencies constantly review the credit quality of firms they have rated. As might be expected, the credit rating of many companies will fluctuate over time as they experience changes in their corporate well-being. As a guide to the change in credit rating that might be expected over a 1-year period, Moody's and S&P publish historical transition matrices, which provide the average rating transition probabilities for each class of rating. An example is shown at Table 8.1, which is Moody's 1-year ratings transition matrix for 2002. These results are obtained from a sample

Table 8.1   Moody's 1-year rating transition matrix (%).

	Aaa	Aa	A	Baa	Ba	B	Caa	Default
Aaa	93.40	5.94	0.64	0.00	0.02	0.00	0.00	0.00
Aaa	1.61	90.55	7.46	0.26	0.09	0.01	0.00	0.02
Aaa	0.07	2.28	92.44	4.63	0.45	0.12	0.01	0.00
Baa	0.05	0.26	5.51	88.48	4.76	0.71	0.08	0.15
Baa	0.02	0.05	0.42	5.16	86.91	5.91	0.24	1.29
Baa	0.00	0.04	0.13	0.54	6.35	84.22	1.91	6.81
Caa	0.00	0.00	0.00	0.62	2.05	4.08	69.20	24.06

Source: Moody's. Reproduced with permission.

of a large number of firms over many years. In Table 8.1, the first column shows the initial rating and the first row the final rating. For instance, the probability of an A-rated company being downgraded to Baa in 1 year is 4.63%. The probability of the A-rated company defaulting in this year is 0.00%.

There are some inconsistencies in the ratings transition table and this is explained by Moody's as resulting from scarcity of data for some ratings categories. For instance, an Aa-rated company has a 0.02% probability of being in default at year-end, which is higher than the supposedly lower rated A-rated company. Such results must be treated with care. The clearest conclusion from the table is that the most likely outcome at year-end is that the company rating remains the same. It may be that a 1-year time horizon provides little real value; hence, the rating agencies also publish transition matrices for longer periods, such as 5 and 10 years.

We might expect an increased level of default as we move lower down the credit ratings scale. This is borne out in Figure 8.1, which is a reproduction of data published by Moody's. It shows 1-year default rates by credit rating category, for the period 1985–2000. We see that the average 1-year default rate rises from 0 for the highest rated Aaa to 15.7% for the B3 rating category. As we have just suggested

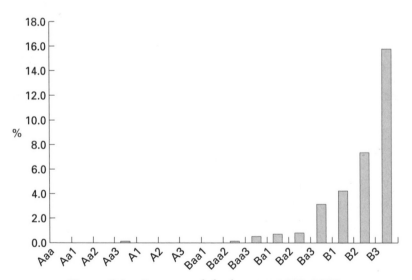

Figure 8.1 One-year default rates 1985–2000.

Source: Moody's. Reproduced with permission.

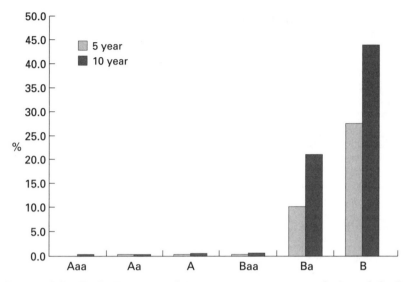

Figure 8.2 Both 5-year and 10-year average cumulative default rates, 1985–2000.

Source: Moody's. Reproduced with permission.

though, some investors attach little value to 1-year results. Figure 8.2 shows average cumulative default rates for 5-year and 10-year time horizons, for the same period covered in Figure 8.1. In fact, this repeats the results shown in Table 8.1, with higher default rates associated with lower credit ratings.

Corporate recovery rates

When a corporate obligor experiences bankruptcy or enters into liquidation or administration, it will default on its loans. However, this does not mean that all the firm's creditors will lose everything. At the end of the administration process, the firm's creditors typically will receive back a portion of their outstanding loans, a *recovery* amount.[1] The percentage of the original loan that is received back is known as the *recovery rate*, which is defined as the percentage of par value that is returned to the creditor.

---

[1] This recovery may be received in the form of other assets, such as securities or physical plant, instead of cash.

Table 8.2 Recovery rates according to loan seniority (%).

Seniority	Mean	Standard deviation
Senior secured bank loans	60.70	26.31
Senior secured	55.83	25.41
Senior unsecured	52.13	25.12
Senior subordinated	39.45	24.79
Subordinated	33.81	21.25
Junior subordinated	18.51	11.26
Preference shares	8.26	10.45

Source: Moody's. Reproduced with permission.

The seniority of a loan strongly influences the level of the recovery rate. Table 8.2 shows recovery rates for varying levels of loan seniority in 2002, as published by Moody's. The standard deviation for each recovery rate reported is high, which illustrates dispersion around the mean and reflects widely varying recovery rates even within the same level of seniority. It is clear that the more senior a loan or a bond is, the higher recovery it will enjoy in the event of default.

CREDIT DERIVATIVES

Credit derivatives have become a major tool for use in managing credit risk exposure. A knowledge of the main credit derivative instruments – credit default swaps (*CDS*) and total return swaps – is essential for risk managers concerned with credit risk. A discussion of the instruments themselves is outside the scope of this book, although we introduce the CDS in Box 8.1.

Box 8.1 The credit default swap

The most common credit derivative is the *credit default swap, credit swap* or *default swap*.[2] This is a bilateral contract in which a periodic fixed fee or a one-off premium is paid to a *protection seller*, in return for which the seller will make a payment on

---

[2] The author prefers the first term, but the other two terms are common. 'Credit swap' does not adequately describe the actual purpose of the instrument.

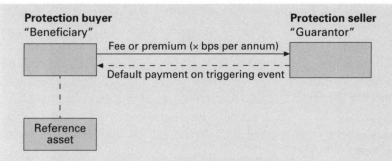

Figure 8.3 Credit default swap.

the occurrence of a specified credit event. The fee is usually quoted as a basis point multiplier of the nominal value. It is usually paid quarterly in arrears, as a per-annum fee.[3] The protection seller is buying the credit risk while the protection buyer is selling credit risk. Since no asset is transferred, there is no need for funding the position – so, the CDS is known as an unfunded credit derivative.

The swap can refer to a single asset (known as the reference entity, reference asset or underlying asset) or a basket of assets. The default payment can be paid in whatever way suits the protection buyer or both counterparties. For example it may be linked to the change in price of the reference asset or another specified asset, it may be fixed at a predetermined recovery rate or it may be in the form of actual delivery of the reference asset at a specified price. Esentially:

$$\text{Pay-out} = 100 - [\text{Recovery value}]$$

Often, the pay-out on a CDS is par minus the market value at the time of default or other credit event.

The basic plain vanilla CDS structure is illustrated at Figure 8.3.

The CDS enables one party to transfer its credit risk exposure to another party. Banks may use default swaps to trade sovereign and

---

[3] The counterparty to the protection seller is, of course, the protection buyer. The protection buyer's position can also be defined as a long put option position on the reference asset, as the bond can be put back to the seller in the event.

corporate credit spreads without trading the actual assets themselves; for example, someone who has gone long a default swap (the protection buyer) will gain if the reference asset obligor suffers a rating downgrade or defaults, and can sell the default swap at a profit if he can find a buyer counterparty. This is because the cost of protection on the reference asset will have increased as a result of the credit event. The original buyer of the default swap need never have owned a bond issued by the reference asset obligor.

As we stated, the default payment on a CDS will be $(1 - \delta)$ times its notional, where δ is defined as the recovery rate of the reference security. The reason for this pay-out is clear – it allows a risky asset to be transformed into a risk-free asset by purchasing default protection referenced to this credit. For example, if the expected recovery rate for a given reference asset is 30% of its face value, upon default the remaining 70% will be paid by the protection seller. Credit agencies such as Moody's and Standard & Poor's provide recovery rate estimates for corporate bonds with different credit ratings using historical data.

The credit default swap contract has a given maturity, but will terminate early if a credit event occurs. The definition of 'credit event' is crucial to the contract and generally is as defined in standard contract documentation. It can include the default of an issuer or an administration or loan restructuring situation. The maturity of the credit swap does not have to match the maturity of the reference asset and often does not. On occurrence of a credit event, the swap contract is terminated and a settlement payment made by the protection seller or guarantor to the protection buyer. This termination value is calculated at the time of the credit event, and the exact procedure that is followed to calculate the termination value will depend on the settlement terms specified in the contract. This will be either cash settlement or physical settlement, as detailed below.

Measuring risk for a CDS contract

Banks calculate a quantitative measure of the risk exposure of their CDS positions. The approach used follows the same VaR principles used for earlier asset class products; namely, it calculates the sensitivity of a contract to variations in market parameters. The main risk measure regards the sensitivity of the CDS to a change in the primary credit curve, and is known as Spread01 or usually 'Credit01'.

Credit01 is a measure of the change in the mark-to-market value of a CDS contract for a 1-bp parallel shift upwards in the credit-risky curve. The precise definition differs depending on whether one is measuring the risk on a bought or sold protection position. The value of a short credit (buy protection) CDS position increases as credit spreads widen, while the value of a long credit (sell protection) position decreases as credit spreads widen. Generally, the market quotes the Credit01 value of a long credit (sold protection) contract as negative, which matches the sign for a short credit position. Essentially, Credit01 is similar in concept to the present value of a basis point $(PVBP)$ or DV01 (Dollar01) interest rate risk measure for a cash bond holding.

The change in the mark-to-market value is given by:

$$\text{Notional} \times \text{Credit01} \times \Delta\text{Spread}$$

with this value being negative or positive depending on whether the holder is buying or selling protection.

There is also an interest rate sensitivity measure for CDS contracts, although this sensitivity is relatively insignificant unless one is experiencing high market volatility. The risk measure of sensitivity to changes in the interest rate yield curve (the Libor curve) is known as IR01 or Libor01, and measures the change in value of the contract for a 1-bp upward parallel shift in the Libor curve.

MODELLING CREDIT RISK

The main credit risk VaR methodologies take a *portfolio* approach to credit risk analysis. This means that:

- the credit risks to each obligor across the portfolio are re-stated on an equivalent basis and aggregated in order to be treated consistently, regardless of the underlying asset class;
- correlations of credit quality moves across obligors are taken into account.

This allows portfolio effects – the benefits of diversification and risks of concentration – to be quantified.

The portfolio risk of an exposure is determined by four factors:

- size of the exposure;
- maturity of the exposure;
- probability of default of the obligor;
- systematic or concentration risk of the obligor.

Credit VaR – like market risk VaR – considers (credit) risk in a mark-to-market framework. It arises from changes in value due to credit events; that is, changes in obligor credit quality including defaults, upgrades and downgrades.

Nevertheless, credit risk is different in nature from market risk. Typically, market return distributions are assumed to be relatively symmetrical and approximated by normal distributions. In credit portfolios, value changes will be relatively small upon minor up/down grades, but can be substantial upon default. This remote probability of large losses produces skewed distributions with heavy downside tails that differ from the more normally distributed returns assumed for market VaR models. This is shown in Figure 8.4.

This difference in risk profiles does not prevent us from assessing risk on a comparable basis. Analytical method market VaR models consider a time horizon and estimate VaR across a distribution of estimated market outcomes. Credit VaR models similarly look to a

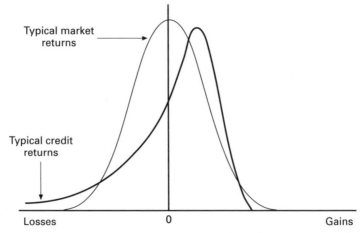

Figure 8.4 Comparison of distribution of market returns and credit returns.

horizon and construct a distribution of value given different estimated credit outcomes.

When modelling credit risk the two main measures of risk are:

- *distribution of loss* – obtaining distributions of loss that may
  arise from the current portfolio. This considers the question of
  what the expected loss is for a given confidence level;
- *identifying extreme or catastrophic outcomes* – this is addressed
  through the use of scenario analysis and concentration limits.

To simplify modelling, no assumptions are made about the causes of
default. Mathematical techniques used in the insurance industry are
used to model the event of an obligor default.

Time horizon

The choice of time horizon will not be shorter than the time frame
over which risk-mitigating actions can be taken. The bank Credit
Suisse First Boston (*CSFB*) (who introduced the CreditRisk$^+$ model)
suggest two alternatives:

- a constant time horizon such as 1 year;
- a hold-to-maturity time horizon.

Data inputs

Modelling credit risk requires certain data inputs; for example,
CreditRisk$^+$ uses the following:

- credit exposures;
- obligor default rates;
- obligor default rate volatilities;
- recovery rates.

These data requirements present some difficulties. There is a lack of
comprehensive default and correlation data, and assumptions need
to be made at certain times.

CREDITMETRICS

CreditMetrics is JP Morgan's portfolio model for analysing credit
risk and was the first such credit VaR model, providing an estimate of

VaR due to credit events caused by upgrades, downgrades and default. A software package known as CreditManager is available that allows users to implement the CreditMetrics methodology.

Methodology

There are two main frameworks in use for quantifying credit risk. One approach considers only two states: default and no-default. This model constructs a binomial tree of default *vs* no-default outcomes until maturity (see Figure 8.5).

The other approach, sometimes called the risk-adjusted return on capital (*RAROC*) approach holds that risk is the observed volatility of corporate bond values within each credit rating category, maturity band and industry grouping. The idea is to track a benchmark corporate bond (or index) which has observable pricing. The resulting estimate of volatility of value is then used to proxy the volatility of the exposure (or portfolio) under analysis.

CreditMetrics sits between these two approaches. The model estimates portfolio VaR at the risk horizon due to credit events that include upgrades and downgrades, rather than just defaults. Thus, it adopts a mark-to-market framework. As shown in Figure 8.6 bonds within each credit rating category have volatility of value due to day-to-day credit spread fluctuations. CreditMetrics assumes that all

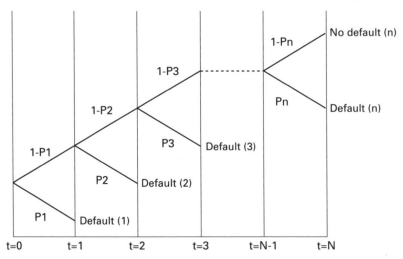

Figure 8.5 A binomial model of credit risk.

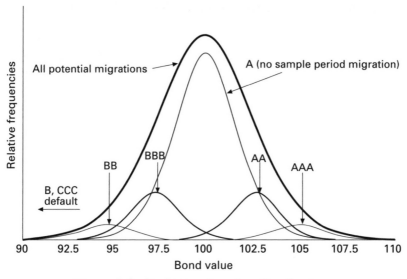

Figure 8.6 Ratings migration distribution.

credit migrations have been realised, weighting each by a migration likelihood.

Time horizon

CreditMetrics adopts a 1-year risk horizon mainly because much academic and credit agency data are stated on an annual basis. This is a convenient convention similar to the use of annualised interest rates in the money markets. The risk horizon is adequate as long as it is not shorter than the time required to perform risk-mitigating actions.

The steps involved in CreditMetrics methodology are shown in Figure 8.7, described by JP Morgan as its analytical 'roadmap'.

The elements in each step are:

- *Exposures*
  - user portfolio;
  - market volatilities;
  - exposure distributions.
- *VaR due to credit events*
  - credit rating;
  - credit spreads;

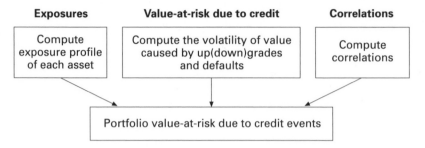

Figure 8.7   Roadmap of the analytics of CreditMetrics.
Source: JP Morgan (1997).

   ○   rating change likelihood;
   ○   recovery rate in default;
   ○   present value bond revaluation;
   ○   Standard deviation of value due to credit quality changes.
- *Correlations*
   ○   ratings series;
   ○   models (e.g., correlations);
   ○   joint credit rating changes.

Calculating the credit VaR

CreditMetrics methodology assesses individual and portfolio VaR due to credit in three steps:

Step 1: It establishes the exposure profile of each obligor in a portfolio.

Step 2: It computes the volatility in value of each instrument caused by possible upgrade, downgrade and default.

Step 3: Taking into account correlations between each of these events it combines the volatility of the individual instruments to give an aggregate portfolio risk.

Step 1   Exposure profiles

CreditMetrics incorporates the exposure of instruments such as bonds (fixed or floating rate) as well as other loan commitments and market-driven instruments, such as swaps. Exposure is stated on an equivalent basis for all products. Products covered include:

- receivables (or trade credit);
- bonds and loans;
- loan commitments;
- letters of credit;
- market-driven instruments.

Step 2 Volatility of each exposure from up(down)grades and defaults

The levels of likelihood are attributed to each possible credit event of upgrade, downgrade and default. The probability that an obligor will change over a given time horizon to another rating is calculated. Each change (migration) results in an estimated change in value (derived from credit spread data and, in default, recovery rates). Each value outcome is weighted by its likelihood to create a distribution of value across each credit state, from which each asset's expected value and volatility (standard deviation) of value are calculated.

There are three stages to calculating the volatility of value in a credit exposure:

- the senior unsecured credit rating of the issuer determines the chance of either defaulting or migrating to any other possible credit quality state in the risk horizon;
- revaluation at the risk horizon can be by either (i) the seniority of the exposure, which determines its recovery rate in case of default, or (ii) the forward zero-coupon curve (spot curve) for each credit rating category which determines the revaluation upon up(down)grade;
- the probabilities from the two steps above are combined to calculate volatility of value due to credit quality changes.

Example 8.1 Calculating probabilities.

An example of calculating the probability step is given below. The probabilities of all possible credit events on an instrument's value must be established first. Given these data the volatility of value due to credit quality changes for this one position can be calculated. The process is shown in Figure 8.8.

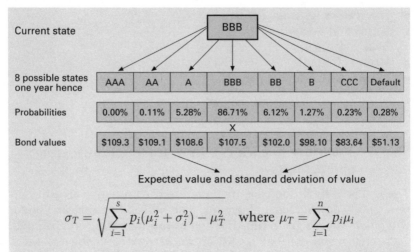

$$\sigma_T = \sqrt{\sum_{i=1}^{s} p_i(\mu_i^2 + \sigma_i^2) - \mu_T^2} \quad \text{where } \mu_T = \sum_{i=1}^{n} p_i\mu_i$$

Figure 8.8 Constructing the distribution value for a BBB-rated bond.

Source: JP Morgan (1997).

Step 3   Correlations

Individual value distributions for each exposure are combined to give a portfolio result. To calculate the portfolio value from the volatility of individual asset values requires estimates of correlation in credit quality changes. CreditMetrics itself allows for different approaches to estimating correlations including a simple constant correlation. This is because of frequent difficulty in obtaining directly observed credit quality correlations from historical data.

CreditManager

CreditManager is the software implementation of CreditMetrics as developed by JP Morgan. It is a PC-based application that measures and analyses credit risk in a portfolio context. It measures the VaR exposure due to credit events across a portfolio, and also quantifies concentration risks and the benefits of diversification by incorporating correlations (following the methodology utilised by Credit-Metrics). The CreditManager application provides a framework for portfolio credit risk management that can be implemented 'off-the-shelf' by virtually any institution. It uses the following:

- obligor credit quality database – details of obligor credit ratings, transition and default probabilities, industries and countries;
- portfolio exposure database – containing exposure details for the following asset types: loans, bonds, letters of credit, total return swaps, CDS, interest rate and currency swaps and other market instruments;
- frequently updated market data – including yield curves, spreads, transition and default probabilities;
- flexible risk analyses with user-defined parameters – supporting VaR analysis, marginal risk, risk concentrations, event risk and correlation analysis;
- stress-testing scenarios – applying user-defined movements to correlations, spreads, recovery rates, transition and default probabilities;
- customised reports and charts.

CreditManager data sources include Dow Jones, Moody's, Reuters, and Standard & Poor's. By using the software package, risk managers can analyse and manage credit portfolios based on virtually any variable, from the simplest end of the spectrum – single position or obligor – to more complex groupings containing a range of industry and country obligors and credit ratings.

Generally, this quantitative measure is employed as part of an overall risk management framework that retains traditional, qualitative methods.

CreditMetrics can be a useful tool for risk managers seeking to apply VaR methodology to credit risk. The model enables risk managers to apply portfolio theory and VaR methodology to credit risk. It has several applications including prioritising and evaluating investment decisions and, perhaps most important, setting risk-based exposure limits. Ultimately, the model's sponsors claim its use can aid maximising shareholder value based on risk-based capital allocation. This should then result in increased liquidity in credit markets, the use of a marking-to-market approach to credit positions and closer interweaving of regulatory and economic capital.

CreditRisk+

CreditRisk+ was developed by CSFB and can in theory handle all instruments that give rise to credit exposure including bonds, loans commitments, letters of credit and derivatives.

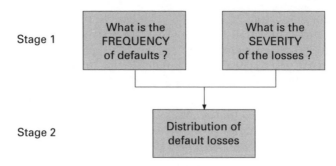

Figure 8.9   CreditRisk⁺ modelling methodology.

The modelling process

CreditRisk⁺ uses a two-stage modelling process as illustrated in Figure 8.9.

CreditRisk⁺ considers the distribution of the number of default events in a time period, such as 1 year, within a portfolio of obligors having a range of different annual probabilities of default.

The annual probability of default of each obligor can be determined by its credit rating and then mapping between default rates and credit ratings. A default rate can then be assigned to each obligor (an example of what this would look like is shown in Table 8.3). Default rate volatilities can be observed from historic volatilities.

Correlation and background factors

Default correlation impacts the variability of default losses from a portfolio of credit exposures. CreditRisk⁺ incorporates the effects

Table 8.3   One-year default rates (%).

Credit rating	One-year default rate
Aaa	0.00
Aa	0.03
A	0.01
Baa	0.12
Ba	1.36
B	7.27

Source: CSFB.

of default correlations by using default rate volatilities and sector analysis.

Unsurprisingly enough, it is not possible to forecast the exact occurrence of any one default or the total number of defaults. Often there are background factors that may cause the incidence of default events to be correlated, even though there is no causal link between them. For example, an economy in recession may give rise to an unusually large number of defaults in one particular month, which would increase the default rates above their average level. CreditRisk$^+$ models the effect of background factors by using default rate volatilities rather than by using default correlations as a direct input. Both distributions give rise to loss distributions with fat tails.

Concentration

As noted above there are background factors that affect the level of default rates. For this reason it is useful to capture the effect of concentration in particular countries or sectors. CreditRisk$^+$ uses a sector analysis to allow for concentration. Exposures are broken down into an obligor-specific element independent of other exposures, as well as non-specific elements that are sensitive to particular factors, such as countries or sectors.

Distribution of the number of default events

CreditRisk$^+$ models the underlying default rates by specifying a default rate and a default rate volatility. This aims to take account of the variation in default rates. The effect of using volatility is illustrated in Figure 8.10, which shows the distribution of default rates generated by the model when rate volatility is varied. The distribution becomes skewed to the right when volatility is increased.

This is an important result and demonstrates the increased risk represented by an extreme number of default events. By varying the volatility in this way, CreditRisk$^+$ is attempting to model for real-world shock much in the same way that market risk VaR models aim to allow for the fact that market returns do not follow exact normal distributions, as shown by the incidence of market crashes.

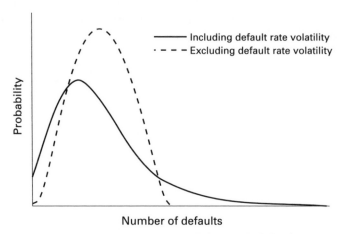

Figure 8.10   CreditRisk$^+$ distribution of default events

Application software

CSFB has released software that allows the CreditRisk$^+$ model to be run on Microsoft Excel® as a spreadsheet calculator. The user inputs his portfolio statistics into a blank template and the model will calculate his credit exposure. Obligor exposure can be analysed on the basis of all exposures being part of the same sector; alternatively, up to eight different sectors (government, countries, industry and so on) can be analysed. The spreadsheet template allows the user to include up to 4,000 obligors in the static data. An example portfolio of 25 obligors and default rates and default rate volatilities (assigned via a sample of credit ratings) is included with the spreadsheet.

The user's static data for the portfolio will therefore include details of each obligor, the size of the exposure, the sector for that obligor (if not all in a single sector) and default rates. An example of static data is given in Tables 8.4 and 8.5.

An example credit loss distribution calculated by the model is shown in Figure 8.11, which shows the distribution for the basic analysis for a portfolio at the simplest level of assumption; all obligors are assigned to a single sector. The full loss distribution over a 1-year time horizon is calculated together with percentiles of the loss distribution (not shown here), which assess the relative risk for different levels of loss. The model can calculate distributions for a portfolio with obligors grouped across different sectors, as well as the

Table 8.4   Example default rate data (%).

Credit rating	Mean default rate	Standard deviation
A+	1.50	0.75
A	1.60	0.80
A−	3.00	1.50
BBB+	5.00	2.50
BBB	7.50	3.75
BBB−	10.00	5.00
BB	15.00	7.50
B	30.00	15.00

Table 8.5   Obligor details.

Company name	Exposure	Rating	Mean default rate	Default rate standard deviation	Sector split General economy
	(£)		(%)	(%)	(%)
Co. (1)	358,475	B	30.00	15.00	100
Co. (2)	1,089,819	B	3.00	15.00	100
Co. (3)	1,799,710	BBB−	10.00	5.00	100
Co. (4)	1,933,116	BB	15.00	7.50	100
Co. (5)	2,317,327	BB	15.00	6.50	100
Co. (6)	2,410,929	BB	15.00	7.50	100
Co. (7)	2,652,184	B	30.00	15.00	100
Co. (8)	2,957,685	BB	15.00	7.50	100
Co. (9)	3,137,989	BBB+	5.00	2.50	100
Co. (10)	3,204,044	BBB+	5.00	2.50	100

distribution for a portfolio analysed over a 'hold to maturity' time horizon.

Summary of the CreditRisk+ Model

- CreditRisk+ captures the main characteristics of credit default events – credit default events are rare and occur in a random manner with observed default rates varying from year to year. The model's approach attempts to reflect this by making no

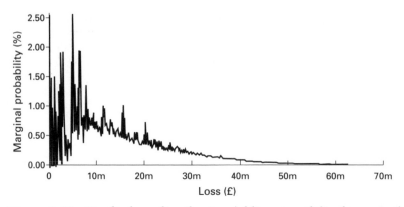

Figure 8.11 Credit loss distribution (obligor portfolio for a single sector).

assumptions about the timing or causes of these events and by incorporating a default rate volatility. It also takes a portfolio approach and uses sector analysis to allow for concentration risk.
*   *CreditRisk+ is capable of handling large exposure portfolios –* the low data requirements and minimum assumptions make the model comparatively easy to implement for firms.

However, the model is limited to two states of the world: default or non-default, as such it is not as flexible as CreditMetrics and, ultimately therefore, not modelling the full exposure that a credit portfolio would be subject to.

APPLICATIONS OF CREDIT VaR

Prioritising risk-reducing actions

One purpose of a risk management system is to direct and prioritise actions. When considering risk-mitigating actions there are various features of risk worth targeting, including obligors having:

*   the largest absolute exposure;
*   the largest percentage level of risk (volatility);
*   the largest absolute amount of risk.

A CreditMetrics methodology helps to identify these areas and allow the risk manager to prioritise risk-mitigating action.

Exposure limits

Within bank dealing desks, credit risk limits are often based on intuitive, but arbitrary, exposure amounts. This is not a logical approach because resulting decisions are not risk-driven. Limits should ideally be set with the help of a quantitative analytical framework.

Risk statistics used as the basis of VaR methodology can be applied to limit setting. Ideally, such a quantitative approach should be used as an aid to business judgement and not as a stand-alone limit setting tool.

A credit committee considering limit setting can use several statistics, such as marginal risk and standard deviation or percentile levels. Figure 8.12 illustrates how marginal risk statistics can be used to make credit limits sensitive to the trade-off between risk and return.

The lines on Figure 8.12 represent risk/return trade-offs for different credit ratings, from AAA to BB. The diagram shows how marginal contribution to portfolio risk increases geometrically with exposure size of an individual obligor, noticeably so for weaker credits. To maintain a constant balance between risk and return, proportionately more return is required with each increment of exposure to an individual obligor.

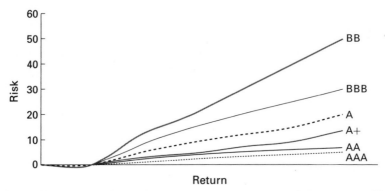

Figure 8.12   Size of total exposure to obligor – risk/return profile.

Standard credit limit setting

In order to equalise a firm's risk appetite between obligors as a means of diversifying its portfolio a credit limit system could aim to have a large number of exposures with equal expected losses. The *expected loss* for each obligor can be calculated as:

Default rate × (Exposure amount − Expected recovery)

This means that individual credit limits should be set at levels that are inversely proportional to the default rate corresponding to the obligor rating.

Concentration limits

Concentration limits identified by CreditRisk$^+$-type methodologies have the effect of trying to limit the loss from identified scenarios and are used for managing 'tail' risk.

INTEGRATING THE CREDIT RISK AND MARKET RISK FUNCTIONS

It is logical for banks to integrate credit risk and market risk management for the following reasons:

- the need for comparability between returns on market and credit risk;
- the convergence of risk measurement methodologies;
- the transactional interaction between credit and market risk;
- the emergence of hybrid credit and market risk product structures.

The objective is for returns on capital to be comparable for businesses involved in credit and market risk, to aid strategic allocation of capital.

Example 8.2 Integrated risk management.

Assume that at the time of annual planning a bank's lending manager says his department can make £5 million over the year if they can increase their loan book by £300 million, while the trading manager says they can also make £5 million if the position limits are increased by £20 million.

Assuming that due to capital restriction only one option can be chosen, which should it be? The ideal choice is the one giving the higher return on capital, but the bank needs to work out how much capital is required for each alternative. This is a quantitative issue that calls for the application of similar statistical and analytical methods to measure both credit and market risk, if one is to compare like with like.

With regard to the loan issue in the example above the expected return is the mean of the distribution of possible returns. Since the revenue side of a loan – that is, the spread – is known with certainty the area of concern is the expected credit loss rate. This is the mean of the distribution of possible loss rates, estimated from historic data based on losses experienced with similar quality credits.

In the context of market price risk the common denominator measure of risk is volatility (the statistical standard deviation of the distribution of possible future price movements). To apply this to credit risk, the decision maker therefore needs to take into account the standard deviation of the distribution of possible future credit loss rates, thereby comparing like with like.

We have shown that as VaR was being adopted as a market risk measurement tool, the methodologies behind it were steadily applied to the next step along the risk continuum, that of credit risk. Recent market events, such as bank trading losses in emerging markets and the meltdown of the Long Term Capital Management hedge fund in summer 1998, have illustrated the interplay between credit risk and market risk. The ability to measure market and credit risk in an integrated model would allow for a more complete picture of the underlying risk exposure. (We would add that adequate senior management understanding and awareness of a third type of risk – liquidity risk – would almost complete the risk measurement picture.)

Market risk VaR measures can adopt one of the different methodologies available; in all of them there is a requirement for estimation of the distribution of portfolio returns at the end of a holding period. This distribution can be assumed to be normal, which allows for analytical solutions to be developed. The distribution may also be estimated using historical returns. Finally, a Monte

Carlo simulation can be used to create a distribution based on the assumption of certain stochastic processes for the underlying variables. The choice of methodology is often dependent on the characteristics of the underlying portfolio plus other factors. For example, risk managers may wish to consider the degree of *leptokurtosis* in the underlying asset returns distribution, the availability of historical data or the need to specify a more sophisticated stochastic process for the underlying assets. The general consensus is that Monte Carlo simulation, while the most IT-intensive methodology, is the most flexible in terms of specifying an integrated market and credit model.

Earlier sub-sections in this section have shown that credit risk measurement models generally fall into two categories. The first category includes models that specify an underlying process of default. In these models firms are assumed to move from one credit rating to another with specified probabilities. Default is one of the potential states that a firm could move to. The CreditMetrics model is of this type. The second type of model requires the specification of a stochastic process for firm value. Here default occurs when the value of the firm reaches an externally specified barrier. In both models, when the firm reaches default the credit exposure is impacted by the recovery rate. Again market consensus would seem to indicate that the second type of methodology, the firm value model, most easily allows for development of an integrated model that is linked not only through correlation but also the impact of *common* stochastic variables.

CASE STUDY
AND EXERCISES

· ·

CASE STUDY – MARKET RISK PROFILE

The following describes the market risk profile, value-at-risk (VaR)
limits and product profile in place for the investment banking arm of
a UK bank in the 1990s. The firm engages in trading worldwide in a
wide range of products, and its use of VaR as a risk measurement tool
is part of a comprehensive risk management framework. The data are
sourced from the bank itself and are reproduced with permission.

VaR allocations

The following table shows the VaR limit allocation across the trading
arm's product range.

	Global (£m)	*UK/ Europe* (£m)	*North America* (£m)	*Asia/ Pacific* (£m)
Money markets	**16.8**	13.5	2.2	1.1
Interest rate derivatives	**4.4**	2.0	0.3	2.1
Currency derivatives	**4.5**	4.5	—	—
Foreign exchange*	**8.0**	6.0	0.6	1.4
Global limit	**33.7**			

*Includes proprietary trading and emerging markets groups.

VaR utilisation

	VaR allocation (£m)	Average 60-day utilisation (£m)
Money markets	16.8	11.0
Interest rate derivatives	4.4	2.0
Currency derivatives	4.5	3.0
Foreign exchange:	8.0	4.3
Market-making	2.8	1.5
Proprietary trading	3.4	2.5
Emerging markets	1.8	0.3

Jump risk limits

Product area	Currency	Scenario	Jump risk (£m)
Money markets (dependent on shape of yield curve)	GBP	+50-bps parallel shift in yield curve	100 (total money markets)
	G10 currency	+50-bps parallel shift in yield curve	(included in above)
	G25 currency	±100-bps parallel shift in yield curve	(included in above)
Interest rate derivatives	All	±100-bps parallel shift in yield curve	20
Currency derivatives	All	±5% move in spot FX	20
		±3% move in volatility	20
FX market-making	G10	±5% move in spot FX	20
	G25	±10% move in spot FX	
Emerging markets	Global	±5% parallel shift in yield curve	20
		±15% move in spot FX	
Proprietary trading	G10	±50-bps parallel shift in yield curve	15
		±5% move in spot FX	
		±3% move in volatility	
		±5% move in equity index	

Role of the market risk function

The bank has an independent risk management function, called 'group market risk', that reports to the group head of trading risk (a group board member). The department's primary role is to:

- determine appropriate risk limit structures and methodologies;
- monitor limit utilisations;
- escalate trading limit breaches to head of group risk or the business chief executive;
- regularly report risk positions;
- take responsibility for VaR model validation;
- undertake systematic stress-testing and back-testing of the VaR model.

This framework can be considered market best practice and is recommended for banks concerned with managing the risk undertaken as part of their daily operations.

EXERCISES

1. **VaR – analytic method.**

   Calculate the

   (a) 1-day 95% one-tail VaR, and
   (b) the 2-week VaR

   for the following fixed income position:

   Single bond position: 100 lots in **LIFFE** long gilt future.

   Contract size: £100,000 nominal (as of the September 1998 contract; therefore, £1 change in price equals £1,000 change in position value).

   Closing price: 105.75.

   1-year price returns variance: 0.161 604.

   Standard deviation:

   Range over normal:

2. **Portfolio VaR.**

   A simple formula to calculate a one-position 1-day VaR (DVaR) is:

   $$\text{DVaR} = [\text{No. of standard deviations for c.i.}$$
   $$\times \text{Daily volatility}$$
   $$\times \text{Position value}]$$

   For a 99% one-tailed test the number of standard deviations is 2.33.

   Position in £100m 10-year gilt. The daily volatility is 0.71% (equivalent to 11.23% annual volatility, which is the daily figure multiplied by $\sqrt{250}$). Calculate the

   (a) 1-day VaR for this position in isolation, and
   (b) 2-week VaR for the same position.

3. **RiskMetrics example – two-position VaR.**

   Calculate the portfolio VaR using the RiskMetrics™ formulae for the following portfolio:

   Position: A trader is long £10m 10-year gilts and short £20m 5-year gilts.
   Market/Risk: 10-year volatility: 0.999%
                   5-year volatility: 0.632%
                   Correlation: 0.47%

   Volatility here is defined as 'the % of value which may be lost with a certain probability' – for RiskMetrics™ this is 95%. Calculating on this basis, therefore, already takes into account the number of standard deviations used in the VaR equation (unlike in the previous exercise).

   Calculate the individual position VaRs, the undiversified risk (assuming perfect correlation) and then the portfolio VaR.

   What is the diversification benefit to the trader?

Answers

1. Standard deviation: $\sqrt{0.161\,604} = 0.402$.

    Range: $1.645 \times 0.402 = 0.661\,29$.

    (a) 1-day VaR: $0.66/100 \times 105.75 \times £1,000 = £697.95$ for one lot – for 100 lots the 1-day VaR is therefore £69,795.

    (b) 2-week VaR: $\sqrt{10} \times £34,897.5 = £220,711.2$.

2. (a) $\text{DVaR} = 2.33 \times 0.71\% \times £100\text{m}$

    $\qquad = £1.6543\text{m}$

    (b) 2-week VaR $= \sqrt{10} \times £1.6543$

    $\qquad = £5.231\text{m}$.

3. $VaR = Amount\ of\ position \cdot Volatility$

    $$VaR_{port} = \sqrt{VaR_1^2 + VaR_2^2 + 2\rho VaR_1 VaR_2}$$

    10-year bond risk $= £10\text{m} * 0.999\%$

    $\qquad = £99,900$

    5-year bond risk $= £20\text{m} * 0.632\%$

    $\qquad = £126,400$.

    The undiversified risk is simply the sum of the individual risks, which here is £226,300 (this assumes perfect correlation).

    Portfolio risk

    $$= \sqrt{(99,900)^2 + (126,400)^2 + 2(0.47) \times (99,900) \times (126,400)}$$

    $$= £194,490$$

    The diversified risk is calculated using the formula above, and the difference between the two is the diversification benefit to the trader due to correlation. Here it is £226,300 minus £194,490, which is £31,810.

Further questions

A bond portfolio has a 1-day VaR measure of £1m. The market has been observed to be following an autocorrelation trend of 0.10. Calculate the 2-day VaR using:

$$\sigma_{2\text{-day}} = \sqrt{\sigma_{1\text{-day}}^2 + \sigma_{1\text{-day}}^2 + 2\sigma_{1\text{-day}}^2 \rho}$$

The cumulative probability of a B-rated counterparty defaulting over the next 12 months is approximately 6.00%. From your observation of the graph, what is the expected probability of the counterparty defaulting in the first month?

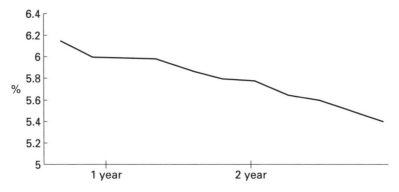

To fulfil regulatory requirements, a risk manager converts a 1-day holding period VaR measure to a 10-day holding period. How would he do this?

What requirements are stipulated by the Basel Committee for banks wishing to calculate VaR for their trading books?

What methodology is JP Morgan's RiskMetrics based on?

A bank calculates its overnight VaR measure to be £12.85m, given a 95% confidence interval. What is the appropriate interpretation of this measure?

Estimate the approximate VaR of a $23m long position in a 10-year Brady bond if the 10-year volatility level is 5.78%.

A bond portfolio has a 1-day VaR measure, at 95% confidence, of $1m. How would you convert this measure to meet Basel Committee VaR measure requirements? What would the equivalent VaR measure be?

ABC Bank plc calculates its VaR with more observations and a higher confidence level (99%, as opposed to 95%) than XYZ Bank plc. Which bank is likely to have a smaller measurement error due to sampling variation?

From the following observations of returns, what is the correlation between A and B?

A: 20, 18, 16, 14, 12, 10
B: 10, 12, 18, 14, 16, 20

The VaR of one instrument is 1,000, while that of another instrument is 800. The combined VaR of both instruments is 1,200. What is the correlation between the instruments? (*Hint*: Use the portfolio variance equation.)

APPENDIX:
TAYLOR'S EXPANSION

· ·

Taylor's Expansion is an important technique in mathematics and was used by Frederick Macaulay when he developed the duration concept for bonds. It was also used by Black and Scholes when they formulated their option pricing model. Latterly, it has been used in developing the delta–gamma approximation for value-at-risk (*VaR*) measurement.

Taylor's Expansion is given by:

$$\Delta G = \frac{dG}{dx} \Delta x + \frac{1}{2} \frac{d^2 G}{dx^2} \Delta x^2 + \frac{1}{6} \frac{d^3 G}{dx^3} \Delta x^3 + \cdots$$

This is, in effect, a calculus differentiation. The first term is the first derivative and can be viewed as the duration of a bond, derived from the price formula. The second term is the second derivative, which is what convexity is in relation to the bond price formula. The third term has little practical impact because it is materially insignificant, so in financial markets it is not considered.

Applying Taylor's Expansion enables us to derive the duration and convexity formulae from the bond price equation. The price of a bond is the present value of all its cash flows, discounted at the appropriate internal rate of return (which becomes the yield to maturity). It is given by:

$$P = \frac{C}{(1+r)} + \frac{C}{(1+r)^2} + \frac{C}{(1+r)^3} + \cdots + \frac{C}{(1+r)^n} + \frac{M}{(1+r)^n} \quad \text{(A1.1)}$$

assuming complete years to maturity paying annual coupons, and with no accrued interest at the calculation date. If we take the first derivative of this expression we obtain:

$$\frac{dP}{dr} = \frac{(-1)C}{(1+r)^2} + \frac{(-2)C}{(1+r)^3} + \cdots + \frac{(-n)C}{(1+r)^{n+1}} + \frac{(-n)M}{(1+r)^{n+1}} \quad (A1.2)$$

If we re-arrange (A1.2) we will obtain the expression (A1.3), which is our equation to calculate the approximate change in price for a small change in yield:

$$\frac{dP}{dr} = -\frac{1}{(1+r)} \left[\frac{1C}{(1+r)} + \frac{2C}{(1+r)^2} + \cdots + \frac{nC}{(1+r)^n} + \frac{nM}{(1+r)^n} \right] \quad (A1.3)$$

The expression above gives us the approximate measure of the change in price for a small change in yield. If we divide both sides of (A1.3) by P we obtain the expression for the approximate percentage price change, given at (A1.4):

$$\frac{dP}{dr}\frac{1}{P} = -\frac{1}{(1+r)} \left[\frac{1C}{(1+r)} + \frac{2C}{(1+r)^2} + \cdots + \frac{nC}{(1+r)^n} + \frac{nM}{(1+r)^n} \right] \frac{1}{P} \quad (A1.4)$$

If we divide the bracketed expression in (A1.4) by the current price of the bond P we obtain the definition of Macaulay Duration:

$$D = \frac{\dfrac{1C}{(1+r)} + \dfrac{2C}{(1+r)^2} + \cdots + \dfrac{nC}{(1+r)^n} + \dfrac{nM}{(1+r)^n}}{P} \quad (A1.5)$$

Equation (A1.5) is frequently re-written as:

$$D = \frac{\displaystyle\sum_{n=1}^{N} \frac{nC_n}{(1+r)^n}}{P} \quad (A1.6)$$

where C represents the bond cash flow at time n, or as:

$$D = \frac{C}{P} \sum_{n=1}^{N} \frac{n}{(1+r)^n} + \frac{M}{P} \frac{N}{(1+r)^N} \quad (A1.7)$$

where $n =$ Time in years to the nth cash flow;
             $N =$ Time to maturity in years.

This is obviously measuring the same thing, but the expression has been re-arranged in a slightly different way.

The markets commonly use a measure of bond price sensitivity to interest rates[1] known as *modified duration*. If we substitute the expression for Macaulay Duration (A1.5) into equation (A1.6) for the approximate percentage change in price we obtain (A1.8):

$$\frac{dP}{dr}\frac{1}{P} = -\frac{1}{(1+r)}D \tag{A1.8}$$

This is the definition of modified duration, given as (A1.9):

$$MD = \frac{D}{(1+r)} \tag{A1.9}$$

So, modified duration is clearly related to duration; in fact, we can use it to indicate that, for small changes in yield, a given change in yield results in an inverse change in bond price. We can illustrate this by substituting (A1.9) into (A1.8), giving us (A1.10):

$$\frac{dP}{dr}\frac{1}{P} = -MD \tag{A1.10}$$

Taking the second derivative of the duration expression and again dividing by the bond price P gives us the formula for convexity. Note that the second term in the Taylor Expansion contains the coefficient $\frac{1}{2}$. Hence, we multiply the convexity by $\frac{1}{2}$ to obtain the convexity adjustment.

With respect to options, the Taylor Expansion is applied the same way; the first term is the equivalent of delta while the second term is the equivalent of gamma. That is, delta and gamma are the first and second derivatives of the Black–Scholes pricing formula.

---

[1] Referred to as *interest rate sensitivity* or interest rate *risk*.

ABBREVIATIONS

....

BIS	Bank for International Settlements
BoE	Bank of England
bp, bps	Basis point(s)
B-S model	Black–Scholes option pricing model
CAD	Capital Adequacy Directive
CDS	Credit Default Swap
Charisma	*Cha*se *Ri*sk *M*anagement *A*nalyser
c.i.	Confidence interval
CP	Commercial Paper
CSFB	Credit Suisse First Boston
DEaR	Daily Earnings at Risk
EMU	European Monetary Union
EU	European Union
FRA	Forward Rate Agreement
FRR	Financial Resources Requirement
FSA	Financial Services Authority
FX	Foreign eXchange
GARCH	Generalised AutoRegressive Conditional Heteroscedasticity (model)
LIBOR, Libor	London Interbank Offered Rate
LIFFE	London International Financial Futures and Options Exchange
OTC	Over The Counter
p&l	Profit and loss
PVBP	Present Value of a Basis Point
RAROC	Risk Adjusted Return On Capital
SFA	Securities and Futures Authority
VaR	Value at Risk
YTM	Yield To Maturity

SELECTED
BIBLIOGRAPHY

BoE (1996). *Working Paper No. 79*. Bank of England.
BoE (1998). *Quarterly Bulletin*. Bank of England.
Beder, T. S. (1995). Analysis VaR. *Financial Analysts Journal*, Sept./Oct.
Blake, D. (2000). *Financial Market Analysis* (2nd edn). FT Prentice Hall.
Bessis, J. (2002). *Risk Management in Banking* (2nd edn). John Wiley & Sons.
Butler, C. (1999). *Mastering Value-at-Risk*. FT Pitman.
Choudhry, M. (2004). *Fixed Income Markets: Instruments, Applications, Mathematics*. John Wiley & Sons.
CSFB (1997). *CreditRisk+*. Credit Suisse First Boston.
Eales, B. and Choudhry, M. (2003). *Derivative Instruments*. Butterworth Heinemann.
Financial Analysts Journal, Sept./Oct. 1995.
Joon, K. and Ramaswamy, K. (1993) Does default risk in coupons affect the valuation of corporate bonds?: A contingent claims model. *Financial Management*, **117**, Autumn.
JP Morgan (1997). *Introduction to CreditMetrics*.
Kolb, R. (2000). *Futures, Options and Swaps* (3rd edn), Blackwell.
Macaulay, F. (1938 [2000]). *Interest Rates, Bond Yields and Stock Prices in the United States since 1856*. RISK Classics Library.
MIT Study (1996). *The New VaR Methodology*. MIT Press.
SFA (1998). *Board Notice 458*, Feb.
Smitson, P. and Minton, D. (1997). *Risk*, February.
University of Reading ISMA Centre (1996). *Risk Management in International Securities Markets: Are Today's Standards Appropriate?*
Wisniewski, M. (1994). *Quantitative Methods for Decision Makers*. Pitman.

INDEX

Other titles by the author

··

Corporate Bond Markets: Instruments and Applications, John Wiley & Sons, 2005.

The Money Markets Handbook: A Practitioner's Guide, John Wiley & Sons, 2005.

Structured Credit Products: Credit Derivatives and Synthetic Securitisation, John Wiley & Sons, 2004.

Advanced Fixed Income Analysis, Elsevier, 2004.

Handbook of European Fixed Income Securities (editor, with Frank Fabozzi), John Wiley & Sons, 2004.

Analysing and Interpreting the Yield Curve, John Wiley & Sons, 2004.

The Gilt-Edged Market, Butterworth-Heinemann, 2003.

Derivative Instruments (with Brian Eales), Butterworth-Heinemann, 2003.

The Repo Handbook, Butterworth-Heinemann, 2002.

Capital Market Instruments: Analysis and Valuation, FT Prentice Hall, 2001.

Bond Market Securities, FT Prentice Hall, 2001.

The Bond and Money Markets: Strategy, Trading, Analysis, Butterworth-Heinemann, 2001.